SINGER

SEWING REFERENCE LIBRARY®

Tailoring

Cy DeCosse Incorporated
Minnetonka, Minnesota

SINGER

SEWING REFERENCE LIBRARY®

Tailoring

Contents

How to Use This Book 7

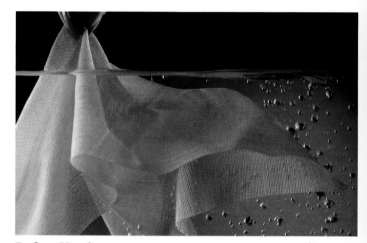

Copyright © 1988
Cy DeCosse Incorporated
5900 Green Oak Drive
Minnetonka, Minnesota 55343
All rights reserved
Printed in U.S.A.

Also available from the publisher: *Sewing
Essentials, Sewing for the Home, Clothing Care
& Repair, Sewing for Style, Sewing Specialty
Fabrics, Sewing Activewear, The Perfect Fit,
Timesaving Sewing, More Sewing for the Home,
Sewing Update 1988*

Library of Congress
Cataloging-in-Publication Data

Tailoring
p. cm. — (Singer sewing reference library)
Includes index.
ISBN 0-86573-241-8
ISBN 0-86573-242-6 (pbk.)
1. Coats. 2. Tailoring (Women's)
I. Cy DeCosse Incorporated. II. Series.
TT535.T35   1988   646'.457—dc19
88-9559 CIP

Distributed by: Contemporary Books, Inc.,
  Chicago, Illinois

CY DE COSSE INCORPORATED
Chairman: Cy DeCosse
President: James B. Maus
Executive Vice President: William B. Jones

TAILORING
Created by: The Editors of Cy DeCosse
  Incorporated, in cooperation with the
  Singer Education Department. Singer is a
  trademark of The Singer Company and is
  used under license.

Managing Editor: Reneé Dignan
Editorial Director: Rita Opseth
Project Manager: Melissa Erickson

Art Director: Lisa Rosenthal
Writer: Barbara Weiland O'Connell
Editors: Bernice Maehren, Susan Meyers
Technical Adviser: Phyllis Galbraith
Sample Supervisor: Carol Neumann
Technical Photo Director: Bridget Haugh
Sewing Staff: Phyllis Galbraith, Bridget
  Haugh, Sheila Duffy, Wendy Fedie, Valerie
  Ruthardt, Pamela Steppe, Jeanine Theroux,
  Joanne Wawra
Photo Studio Manager: Cathleen Shannon
Photographers: Rex Irmen, Tony Kubat, John
  Lauenstein, Bill Lindner, Mark Macemon,
  Mette Nielsen

Production Manager: Jim Bindas
Assistant Production Managers: Julie Churchill,
  Jacquie Marx
Production Staff: Janice Cauley, Joe Fahey,
  Carol Ann Kevan, Yelena Konrardy, Christi
  Maybee, Dave Schelitzche, Linda Schloegel,
  Jennie Smith, Greg Wallace, Scott Winton,
  Nik Wogstad
Consultants: LaVern Bell, Zoe Graul,
  Barbara Weiland O'Connell, Jane Schenck,
  Wanda Sieben, Marcy Tilton
Contributing Manufacturers: B. Blumenthal
  & Company; Clotilde; Coats & Clark;
  Crown Textile Company™/Armo Division;

Dritz Corporation; Dyno Merchandise
Corporation; EZ International;
Freudenberg, Pellon Division; House
of Laird; JHB International; June
Tailor, Inc.; Logantex, Inc.; Olfa Products
Corporation; Paco Despacio, Buttonsmith;
Rowenta, Inc.; Seams Great Products,
Inc.; The Singer Company; Stacy
Industries, Inc.; Streamline Industries,
Inc.; Swiss-Metrosene, Inc.
Color Separations: Color Control
Printing: W. A. Kreuger (0488)

How to Use This Book

One of the most satisfying sewing projects is a tailored jacket or coat. *Tailoring* takes you through the process step-by-step. It guides you in selecting the tailoring method most appropriate for your fabric and pattern choice, as well as for your skill level and available sewing time.

Most tailoring procedures are not difficult. Many are used in everyday dressmaking, so progressing to a tailored garment is a natural step. Although "tailored" usually implies a garment with notched collar and lapels and a lining, many of the techniques used to create such a garment are also used in constructing other jacket and coat styles, including unlined ones.

Custom tailoring was once the only technique for creating a professionally tailored garment, but now the machine and fusible methods are natural choices when faster, easier construction is desired. All three methods are included in *Tailoring* with suggestions for where and how to use them alone or in combination.

Making Selections

The first section of this book describes the three tailoring methods and explains how to choose garment fabrics, interfacings, lining fabrics, and notions for tailoring. Because some fabrics respond better to tailoring than others, information is included to help you evaluate fabrics and choose only those that are appropriate.

Interfacings and the methods used to apply them make the difference in the appearance of a professionally tailored garment, so you will want to test new techniques and interfacings before using them in a garment. If you choose tailoring with fusible interfacings, be sure to review the fusing directions and the guidelines for selecting and evaluating fusible interfacings.

Tips & Tools

Even if you feel confident about your sewing skills, take the time to review the section on tips and tools before starting your tailoring project. Some of the hand stitches used in tailoring may be new to you. Read about these stitches, and practice those that are unfamiliar before using them in your jacket or coat.

Accurate cutting and marking, precise machine stitching, and careful trimming and pressing are also required to create a beautifully tailored jacket or coat. We have included a listing of the tools helpful for tailoring a garment. You may already have most of these tools, so investment in new tools may be minimal.

Before You Sew

Because a tailored jacket or coat is shaped to the body, you may need to adjust the pattern to fit your figure. *Tailoring* includes fitting guidelines and directions for pin-fitting the pattern and making a test garment to perfect the fit, along with common fitting adjustments for tailored garments.

Professional tailors use specially shaped interfacing pieces to create support and shaping in a tailored garment. Use the directions in this section to cut the interfacing the way tailors do. To ensure that your garment fabric and interfacings are compatible and that the finished garment will endure repeated cleanings without shrinkage, follow the directions for preparing the fabric before cutting and marking.

Tailoring & Finishing Techniques

Most pattern guidesheets are written according to space limitations, and the instructions are generalized to cover a wide range of fabrics and skill levels. For truly professional results, use the pattern instructions as a general guide and supplement them with the more detailed instructions that are included in this book.

The tailoring techniques are organized according to the sequence recommended for constructing a tailored jacket and may vary from the order usually given in the pattern guidesheet. The undercollar is tailored first to give you an idea of how the fabric handles and an opportunity to practice unfamiliar techniques on a smaller piece of fabric before proceeding to the lapels.

Custom tailoring methods are shown first, followed by the faster machine and fusible methods. Even if you select one of the faster methods, read through the custom method first for a better understanding of the shaping technique and desired results. Regardless of the tailoring method you choose, the result will be a beautifully tailored jacket or coat.

Making Selections

The Standards of Tailoring

Tailoring uses advanced techniques and materials to change a flat piece of fabric into a three-dimensional garment with structure and shape. Tailored jackets and coats are molded to body contours with interfacings to create permanent shape in the collar and lapels. Shoulder pads, sleeve heads, and stay tape supplement the interfacing for additional shaping and support. Careful pressing sets the new shape. A lining or partial lining covers the inner construction to extend the wear and to make the garment easier to slide on and off over other clothing.

Traditionally tailored jackets and coats are shaped and structured designs with a notched or shawl collar. Most of the shaping that characterizes a tailored garment is done in this area. But tailoring techniques are also important for building in shape, adding support, and stabilizing other jacket and coat styles, such as collarless cardigan jackets. Some jacket designs combine tailoring and dressmaking techniques to achieve the softly tailored look intended by the designer.

Tailoring Methods

Three methods are available for tailoring a garment: custom, machine, and fusible. Custom tailoring requires the most handwork. Hand stitching, called padstitching, attaches hair canvas interfacing to the collar and lapels as it builds in shape. Although it is the most time-consuming method, custom tailoring has stood the test of time and is as appropriate today as it was in the past. The custom method sets the standard of a fine-quality garment.

When sewing time is limited, choose one of the faster methods; they also produce excellent results. In the machine tailoring method, hair canvas is padstitched by machine instead of by hand. Or use fusible interfacings instead of hair canvas, and eliminate hand or machine padstitching, allowing yourself to complete a tailored garment in even less time. Fusible interfacing may not fuse securely to some fabrics. If you have selected one of these fabrics for a tailored garment and wish to use a fast method of tailoring, select the machine method.

After making a few garments, many tailors find that they prefer one method over another. Others combine custom, machine, and fusible methods, using different methods in different areas of the same garment. For example, you may prefer to shape the collar and lapels using the custom method, yet save time by fusing interfacing in the vent areas and attaching the lining by machine.

Choose the tailoring method that will retain the character of the fabric and will shape the pattern as designed. The custom method provides firm shaping in the collar and lapel area, but allows the softer drape of the fabric to be retained in the body of the garment. This is also true of garments tailored by the machine method; however, the machine stitching may be visible on the undercollar, so this method is not used in collars that are intended to be turned up in the back. When tweed or textured fabrics and closely matched thread are used, this stitching may be barely noticeable.

Beautiful results depend on choosing a figure-flattering pattern, selecting appropriate and easily tailored garment fabrics, and matching them with compatible interfacings and linings. Choosing the tailoring method and fabrics that are most compatible with your available sewing time and your level of sewing skill ensures the best results.

Standards of a Well-tailored Jacket or Coat

Garment has straight, thin edges, sharp corners, and smooth curves, and all handwork is inconspicuous.

Front edges, as well as the finished edges on vents, pocket flaps, and lapels and collar points, roll or cup slightly inward toward the body, never outward.

Seams and darts are smooth and straight with no obvious crooks or puckers.

Facing and hem edges are attached so they do not show from the right side of the finished garment.

Sleeves hang straight without diagonal wrinkles in the sleeve cap.

Lining has enough wearing ease so movement does not cause strain on the fabric.

Buttons fit through buttonholes easily and are lifted away from the garment by shanks to prevent strain and wear on the buttonholes.

Pockets lie flat and fit the curve of the body.

Custom Tailoring Method

A custom-tailored garment is constructed using the traditional method of tailoring. This method is the most time-consuming because it requires a great deal of handwork.

Tailoring Features

Hand padstitching is used to attach the interfacing and to shape the garment.

Hair canvas sew-in interfacing is used to shape the garment front, undercollar, and hems.

Taping the lapel roll line and front edges with stay tape is done by hand.

Lining is inserted by hand.

Fusible Tailoring Method

A garment tailored using fusible interfacing does not require padstitching and is constructed entirely by machine except for setting in the lining sleeves and sewing the hems.

Tailoring Features

Fusible interfacing is used to shape the garment front, front facing, upper collar, undercollar, and hems.

Taping the roll line by machine may be done, but taping the front edges is not necessary.

Lining is inserted by machine, except for the sleeve lining, which is attached by hand.

Machine Tailoring Method

A machine-tailored garment is constructed entirely by machine except for setting in the lining sleeves and sewing the hems.

Tailoring Features

Machine padstitching is used to apply interfacing and to shape the undercollar; lapels may also be padstitched by machine.

Hair canvas sew-in interfacing is used to shape the garment front, undercollar, and hems.

Taping the lapel roll line is done by machine, and taping the front edges is not necessary.

Lining is inserted by machine, except for the sleeve lining, which is attached by hand.

Combination of Methods

A garment may be tailored by combining two or three tailoring methods. Custom, machine, and fusible methods may all be used in the same garment.

Tailoring Features

Hair canvas sew-in interfacing may be selected for undercollar and garment front; fusible interfacing may be selected for the front facing, shoulder reinforcement, upper collar, and hems.

Taping the roll line may be done by the machine method, and taping the front edges by the custom-tailoring method.

Lining may be attached by hand or by machine.

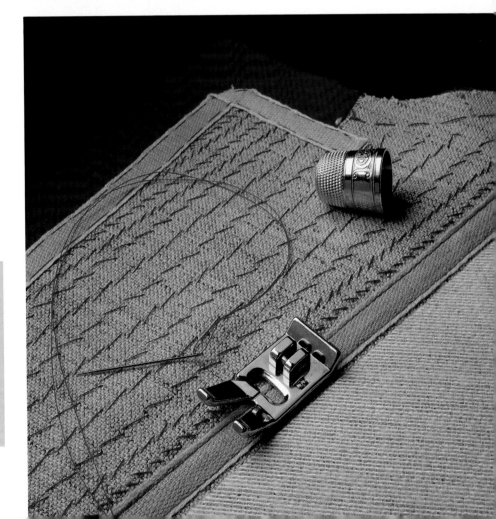

Selecting a Pattern

Research the fashions in magazines, catalogs, boutiques, or department stores to determine whether the current look is soft or more structured. Try on the newest jacket and coat styles at a store to decide which shapes, style details, fabrics, and lengths suit you. Because more time and money are invested in a tailored garment than on other sewing projects, choose a pattern that is current and that will remain fashionable over a period of time. Choose a jacket or coat pattern that will flatter your figure and will build on what is already in your wardrobe.

Although tailoring techniques can be used in a wide variety of jacket and coat styles, there are many features that well-tailored garments often include. For a first tailoring project or when sewing time is limited, choose a jacket with a simpler shawl collar rather than the more complicated notched collar. Some jacket and coat styles have interesting lapel shapes that add style to the garment.

Dolman or raglan sleeve styles also offer easier construction. Patch pockets are easier than welt pockets. Welt pockets are time-consuming and demand careful cutting and precise stitching.

Before buying a pattern, examine the guidesheet to determine the complexity of the pattern. Look at the shapes of the pattern pieces, the layout, and the steps in construction. Check if the roll lines are marked on the pattern tissue or whether you will need to mark them yourself.

Pattern Features for a Tailored Garment

Tailored collar may be notched for traditional tailored look, or shawl style for a softer look.

Bound buttonholes can be used with any pattern. They are a classic feature of a tailored garment.

Tailored pockets, such as single or double welt pockets, are used for fine detailing. Patch pockets may be used in tailored garments for a more casual effect. If the pattern does not include the pocket style you prefer, making a substitution is relatively easy.

Set-in sleeves may have upper and under sleeves for better fit over the elbow.

Seaming details may include a center back seam, as well as an underarm panel with side front and side back seams, for better fitting and shaping.

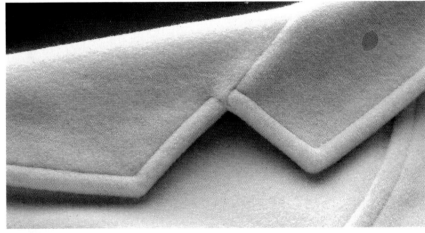

Topstitching may be added to define edges and seamlines.

Full lining allows jacket to slide on easily over other garments. If the pattern is for an unlined or partially lined jacket, a full lining may be substituted.

Sleeve vents and back vents are traditional tailoring details.

Selecting a Tailoring Fabric

Because tailoring takes more time than dressmaking, the garment fabric and labor are the largest investments in a tailored garment. Invest in the highest-quality fabrics that fit within your budget. Higher-quality fabrics are easier to handle, eliminating many sewing problems and frustrations. Tailored garments of better fabrics also wear longer. Evaluate the total cost of the garment and the quality of the fabric rather than the price per yard. With the exception of full-length coats, tailored garments require relatively small yardages.

Characteristics of Tailoring Fabrics

Tailoring techniques are suitable for a wide range of fabrics. Almost any coating or suiting fabric can be tailored with one or more of the methods discussed. For a first tailoring project, a wool fabric with obvious surface texture, such as a tweed, is recommended. Wools respond beautifully to steam pressing and shaping, and stitching irregularities are easily hidden in textured surfaces; however, not all wool fabrics are easy to tailor. Hard-surfaced wool worsteds, such as gabardine, do not ease well, and pressing is more difficult; therefore, they are not recommended for the inexperienced tailor.

For best results, tailoring fabrics should have the characteristics recommended for easier tailoring in the chart on the opposite page. When tailoring a more difficult fabric, plan more time for decision making and testing and more care in stitching and pressing to produce professional results.

Fabrics with obvious designs, such as plaids, stripes, and diagonals, are not recommended for a first tailoring project or when sewing time is limited. Develop skill in matching patterned fabrics in simpler sewing projects before attempting to tailor them. When your fabric choice is more challenging, selecting an easier pattern will save time and simplify the project. Use three quick tests, opposite, to determine how fabrics will respond to sewing and wearing.

Characteristics to Consider When Selecting Tailoring Fabrics

Fabric Characteristic	Fabrics Easier to Tailor	Fabrics More Difficult to Tailor
Fiber content	Natural fibers press and shape well, and can be shrunk to reduce excess ease; stitches blend into fibers.	Synthetic fibers do not shape or ease well, and they scorch or melt easily; removing heat-set creases is difficult.
Color	Medium to medium-dark colors conceal inner construction of garment, such as seams, hems, and interfacing; these colors do not show wear from handling or soiling.	Light colors may allow seams, hems, and interfacings to show through to right side of fabric. Dark colors cause eyestrain; overpressed, shiny surfaces will be more noticeable.
Weight	Mediumweight fabrics press more easily; edges trim well for thin, crisp finish.	Lightweight fabrics are easily overpressed. Heavy fabrics are time-consuming to press; due to bulk, they are hard to manipulate during sewing.
Texture	Fabrics with surface texture and interest hide stitching imperfections. Texture can hide seam edges and edges of interfacing so they do not show through to right side of fabric.	Smooth, hard-finished fabrics show every flaw in workmanship and pressing; they do not ease or shape well. Napped fabrics require special pressing and pattern layout; fusible interfacing cannot be applied to velvets.
Weave	Medium weaves are flexible, hold their shape, do not ravel easily, shape well in easing and pressing, and are easy to manipulate with hand stitching and steam pressing; stitches blend into the fibers.	Loosely woven fabrics may stretch out of shape; they are suitable for fusible method of tailoring, but ravel easily unless fused. Tightly woven fabrics do not shape well; they may needle-mark, and seams may pucker.

Three Tests for Selecting a Tailoring Fabric

Crush the fabric in your hand, and release it to check resilience. If creases or wrinkles remain, fabric will be more difficult to tailor.

Push fabric with your thumbs to check durability. If yarns separate and fabric does not recover its shape, it will stretch out of shape when sewn or worn.

Test fabric drape by placing fabric over bustline. If fabric does not fall into flattering folds, it will be more difficult to tailor.

Tailoring Plaids & Stripes

Plaids and stripes offer special tailoring challenges. If you are an experienced sewer, a plaid or striped jacket or coat may be just the project to further develop your sewing expertise. Matching plaids and stripes during layout, cutting, and sewing can add several hours to the construction of a jacket or coat.

Designs such as houndstooths and herringbones or other woven-in patterns also require matching because the design of the fabric repeats in rows or blocks of color. Random designs do not require matching.

The recommendations that follow are for planning the placement of a plaid. The same guidelines apply for matching stripes. For stripes, consider the placement of either vertical or horizontal lines only, depending on the direction of the stripes in the fabric.

Selecting Patterns & Fabric

If the design is shown in a plaid in the pattern sketch or photograph, you can be sure it is suitable for plaids. Do not consider the pattern if it is described as "unsuitable for plaids and stripes" on the back of

How to Match Designs in a Tailored Jacket or Coat

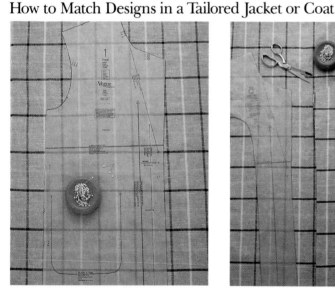

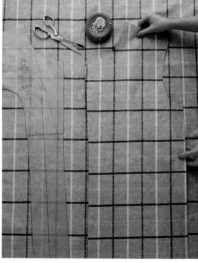

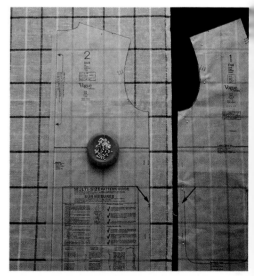

1) Lay out each piece in single layer; begin with jacket front. Position center front on or between two dominant vertical lines. Check position for desired crosswise lines at bust, waist, and hem. Cut single layer of jacket front; remove tissue.

2) Turn over jacket front to use as pattern for matching and cutting second piece. Cut front facing with crosswise lines matching at front edge. Lapel seamline follows dominant vertical line as much as possible; facing may be off-grain.

3) Position center back on or between two dominant vertical lines as for center front. Position pattern on fabric, matching notches (arrows) of front and back pieces at the same point in the plaid design at the *seamline*.

the pattern envelope. Patternmakers include this statement when seam shaping makes it difficult to match the design.

Choose patterns with few seamlines and simple details to avoid breaking up the fabric design. It is rarely possible to match every line at every seamline, but too many seams or areas that do not match are distracting. Whenever possible, avoid horizontal or diagonal bustline darts in plaid jackets. When these darts are present, side seams should match below the dart but will not match above it. If elbow shaping in the sleeve is created with a dart or easing, the lengthwise sleeve seam should match above the dart but will not match below it.

Placement Tips

Making a test garment (pages 50 to 53) is a good idea since it is important to establish finished hem lengths and make any major fitting changes before planning the plaid layout.

Before cutting and layout, decide the placement of plaid design lines within the garment and where they will fall on the body. Avoid placing a dominant horizontal line or block of lines at the bustline and waistline if possible. Experiment with the fabric draped from shoulder to hem. Some plaid garments look more balanced when the hemline falls at the bottom of a dominant crosswise line. If you wish to draw the eye away from the hemline, place the hemline between two dominant lines.

Place dominant vertical lines at the center front and center back, or position the pattern so the center front is halfway between two dominant vertical lines. Position the upper sleeve in the same way, using the shoulder dot as the guide for centering the sleeve on or between the dominant vertical lines.

The plaid may not match at the shoulder seams, the seam where the upper collar meets the lapel, and the back notch in the armhole of a set-in sleeve. Pockets, cuffs, and pocket flaps should be cut after the first fitting because placement may need to be adjusted.

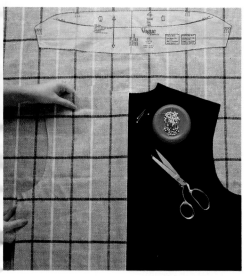

4) Cut around outside edges of back pattern; mark top and bottom of foldline. Remove tissue; fold fabric, matching plaids. Cut around remaining half. Cut upper collar to match at center back.

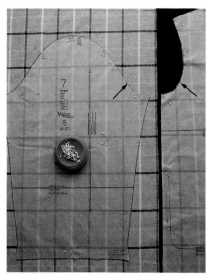

5) Center sleeve on or between dominant vertical lines. Position pattern so plaid matches jacket at front notch (arrows) at *seamline*. Do not force a match at back notch. Cut single layer; turn over sleeve to use as pattern for second sleeve.

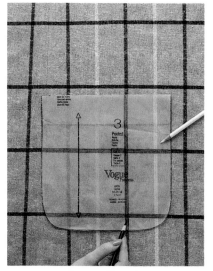

6) Place patch or flap pocket pattern pieces in position on garment at first fitting; pencil in plaid line location for matching. Lay out pockets on fabric; cut.

Interfacings for Tailoring

Interfacing adds body and shape through the shoulders and chest and at the armholes of tailored garments. It supports the back of the garment and adds firmness, stability, and line definition to the front edges or to design details, such as pockets and cuffs. Interfacing also helps produce a smooth roll in the collar and lapels, and cushions hem edges for better wear.

In custom-tailored garments, hair canvas and the garment fabric for the collar and lapels are shaped over your hand. The hair canvas is then sewn to the garment fabric with padstitches. When fusible interfacing is chosen, shaping is achieved with steam pressing.

Decide whether you want to create a softly tailored or more structured garment. This decision depends on personal preference, the current fashion trend, and the pattern you have chosen. Then select the appropriate tailoring method: custom, machine, or fusible tailoring—or a combination. As you experiment with different tailoring methods and interfacing applications in each new garment you make, the choices for future tailoring projects will become easier.

Sew-in Interfacings

For custom tailoring, purchase the best available grade of hair canvas. Hair canvas should be pliable, firmly woven, noncrushable, and resilient. Most hair canvas is a blend of wool, goat hair, and cotton or rayon. A high wool content of at least 30 to 40 percent makes the hair canvas softer, easier to handle, and easier to shape with steam pressing. Goat hair makes the hair canvas resilient and more wrinkle resistant. It also helps the interfacing cling to the garment fabric to make the two fabrics act as one. The hair content should be 7 to 17 percent. High content of rayon or cotton instead of wool reduces the price, but the hair canvas is not as resilient. It also wrinkles more easily and is not as responsive to shaping.

A lightweight woven interfacing back stay supports the back of a tailored jacket or coat (page 56). Choose muslin or broadcloth to blend with or match the garment fabric. When the garment is a simpler style without a collar and lapel, interfacing is necessary for support only, rather than for shaping. Nonwoven or woven sew-in interfacing fabrics other than hair canvas may be used.

Sometimes it is necessary to add another shaping fabric layer to a tailoring fabric before constructing the garment. This layer is called an *underlining*. It lies directly under the garment fabric and is basted to the wrong side of each garment piece; it is applied before the interfacing. Underlining is not recommended unless needed to stabilize an open-weave fabric or to hide seam allowances and inner construction so they do not show through a light-colored garment fabric. Avoid adding an underlining to make a garment fabric more suitable for a structured, tailored garment.

Types of Interfacings for Tailoring

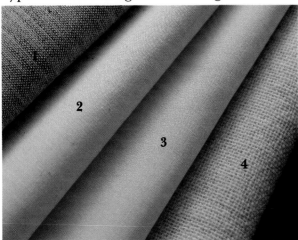

Sew-in interfacings. Use hair canvas (**1**) for shaping the undercollar, lapel, and hems of custom-tailored and machine-tailored garments. A lightweight woven interfacing is used for the back stay; select muslin (**2**) or broadcloth (**3**) to blend with or match the garment fabric. Lambswool (**4**) may be used where soft padding is desired, such as for sleeve heads, or for added warmth as an interlining.

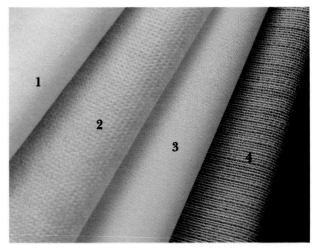

Fusible interfacings. Interfacings used for fusible tailoring are woven (**1**), nonwoven (**2**), knit (**3**), and weft-insertion (**4**). A wide variety of weights is available for firm shaping of structured garments or supple shaping for softer tailoring.

For underlining, select a lightweight woven fabric, such as muslin or broadcloth, and choose the color carefully. Fusible knit interfacings may also be used. Place the garment fabric over the underlining to check for any color change. Underline only the body and sleeves, unless the fabric has a very open weave; then underline the entire garment to prevent a noticeable difference in the color of details.

Fusible Interfacings

Fusible interfacings, which have a heat-activated resin coating on one side, eliminate most of the time-consuming handwork. When applied properly, they provide the same kind of shaping and support as sew-in interfacings.

Fusible interfacings should not be used on fabrics that will be damaged by prolonged heat, pressure, and moisture. They may not fuse permanently to heavily textured fabrics or those with slick, glazed surfaces. Do not use fusible interfacing on fabrics treated for water repellency or stain resistance. These fabrics are treated with silicone, which prevents bonding.

Fusibles are available in a variey of weights and types. There are four categories: woven, nonwoven, knit, and weft-insertion. When comparing interfacings of the same weight from different categories, you will find subtle differences in the way the interfacings drape and roll. Selecting the appropriate weight

of fusible interfacing is more critical than selecting which type of interfacing to use; however, knowing the differences between categories will help you produce the desired effect in a tailored garment. After testing several interfacings, you will be able to feel and see how the interfacing shapes the garment fabric. Select the interfacing that gives the effect you like. Let your personal taste guide you.

Woven fusible interfacings stretch on the bias, but are stable crosswise and lengthwise. The selection of fusible wovens that are suitable for tailoring is limited. Fusible hair canvas is available but may be too stiff when fused to the garment fabric.

Nonwoven fusible interfacings usually have crosswise stretch but no lengthwise stretch. Generally they are less flexible than other interfacings. Some are spongy, enabling them to work well with corduroys and velveteen. All-bias nonwoven fusible interfacings stretch in all directions for greater flexibility.

Fusible knit interfacings have crosswise stretch, but no lengthwise stretch. They provide soft, supple shaping and are more flexible than other fusible interfacings.

Weft-insertion fusible interfacings are stable crosswise and lengthwise, because a yarn is woven in and out of the knit stitches across the fabric. Like woven interfacings, they stretch on the bias. They give firm, yet supple, shaping.

How to Test Sew-in Interfacings

1) Crush a small portion in your hand; then release. Noticeable wrinkles remaining after the fabric relaxes indicate poor resilience.

2) Sandwich interfacing between two layers of the garment fabric to feel the weight and body.

3) Roll interfacing over your hand to determine its flexibility. Fold the layers to simulate the roll of a collar; they should form a soft roll without sharp points or breaks.

Selecting Fusible Interfacing

Because fusible interfacings change the character of the garment fabric and every fabric responds differently, testing is necessary to select the best interfacing for the fabric. Test several types and weights of interfacing on a sample of the garment fabric. To make testing and selection easy and convenient, keep an assortment of fusible interfacings on hand. An assortment will give you the flexibility of using more than one interfacing in a garment. For example, you can use a heavier interfacing for undercollar and lapels, and a lighter one for details and hems.

Before testing the interfacing choices, preshrink the garment fabric and interfacings (page 61). Follow the manufacturer's fusing directions that come with each interfacing. For easy comparison, fuse the interfacing samples to a strip of the garment fabric.

Evaluate test samples, using the guidelines below. Label and save tests for future reference.

After selecting the appropriate interfacing, cut interfacing pieces according to the manufacturer's recommendations for grainline direction because the direction of stretch varies with the type of interfacing. Preheat the iron to the wool setting. Just before fusing, steam press the garment fabric to remove wrinkles and to warm the fabric.

Fuse the interfacing to the garment, following the manufacturer's recommendations for iron temperature, time, pressure, and moisture. The fusing method, opposite, will ensure a perfect bond and can be used as general fusing directions if you do not have the manufacturer's instructions.

Guidelines for Evaluating Fusible Interfacing Tests

Interfacing is securely bonded to fabric. If not, fuse again with more heat, time, and pressure. If fusible interfacing does not adhere securely, use a sew-in interfacing.

Interfacing is smooth. If interfacing bubbles, iron is too hot. Lower the temperature, and increase the fusing time if necessary for smooth bond.

Fabric surface is smooth and pucker-free. If not, fuse again with more time and pressure. Interfacing may be

too heavy for fabric, or heat and moisture may have caused fabric to shrink. Preshrink fabric; test again.

Color has not changed, and there is no visible ridge at cut edge of interfacing. If pinked and straight edges show, interfacing is too heavy for fabric.

Drape and weight are satisfactory. Interfacing should shape fabric with a smooth roll that has a slightly rounded edge. Breaks in the fold indicate that interfacing is too heavy.

How to Test Fusible Interfacings

1) Cut a long strip of garment fabric 6" (15 cm) wide. Cut 3" (7.5 cm) squares of each interfacing; pink one edge of each. Cut small triangle of fabric; tuck under one corner of each interfacing for tab. Fuse interfacing, opposite.

2) Pull fabric tab; try to peel away interfacing. Fabric and interfacing should feel permanently bonded.

3) Fold fabric strip in half over interfacings. Fold each interfacing against itself to simulate layers at front edge of garment. Evaluate test samples, using the chart above.

How to Apply Fusible Interfacing

1) Position interfacing on warm fabric, resin side down; smooth into place. Lightly mist interfacing with water, or steam shrink (page 61). Position press cloth and dampen with liberal misting, even when using steam iron.

2) Start at center of large or long pieces of interfacing, and work toward each end to fuse. Do not slide iron from one position to the next. To ensure complete coverage, overlap fused areas with iron.

3) Use two-handed pressure, and lean on iron; fuse for recommended time, 10 to 15 seconds for most fusible interfacings. Otherwise, bond will not be permanent and will eventually separate from fabric.

4) Press the fused area from right side of fabric for better bonding. Use a press cloth or iron soleplate guard to protect fabric surface. Cool and dry fused fabrics before moving them; interfacing is easily reshaped or distorted while warm.

Selecting Linings

Selecting lining fabric for a tailored garment is as important as selecting the garment fabric. The lining is the finishing touch, covering the inner construction and protecting the garment fabric from unnecessary wear. It also absorbs most of the wearing strain and prevents the jacket from stretching out of shape, particularly where closely fitted.

Linings should be as durable as the garment fabric. Although it is possible to replace a lining that shows signs of wear, it is a time-consuming process. Purchase a high-quality lining that will withstand repeated wearing and drycleaning.

Fiber content and weave are clues to the durability of lining fabrics. Most lining fabrics are made from synthetic fibers. Bemberg® rayon and rayon/acetate blends are recommended because they are more absorbent than other synthetic fibers. They are more comfortable to wear, particularly in hot, humid climates. For this reason, they are particularly appropriate for spring and summer jackets.

Acetate linings may be affected by perspiration and are not as durable as those made of Bemberg rayon. Polyester fibers are very durable but not as absorbent as rayon and acetate, and they are uncomfortable in hot, humid climates. Polyester linings are an excellent choice for coat linings, which are usually subjected to more wear than jacket linings. Silk fibers, although luxurious, are not usually recommended for linings because they are damaged by perspiration.

The lining should be lighter in weight and softer than the garment fabric, with a smooth surface that slides over other fabrics without rustling. Choose one that falls into soft folds when draped over your hand. Test lining choices by sliding them across the garment fabric surface. Avoid textured linings that cling to other garments. For this reason, use the satin side of crepe-back satin as the right side of the lining. The textured crepe side will cling to the garment fabric and hold it in place in the jacket.

Although a jacket or coat lining is on the inside of the finished garment, the edges of the sleeve lining often show or the lining is often visible when you move, so color is an important consideration. The lining color must be dark enough to cover seam and hem edges and inner construction, but not so dark that it shows through to the right side of the garment fabric. The lining color is too light if you can see the interfacing through the lining. Many garment fabrics intended for blouses and dresses are also good for linings. The color range is wider, so matching the lining to the garment fabric is easier.

Fabric weave. Satin (**1**) feels smooth and soft but has float yarns, which snag easily; choose satin weaves with short float yarns. Twill weaves (**2**) are stronger than plain (**3**) and satin weaves. Some lining fabrics have woven jacquard or dobby designs (**4**) created by yarns that float on the surface, forming a pattern. If these designs have long floats, they may catch on watches and jewelry.

Lining color. Choose a solid color (**1**) that matches or blends with the fabric. Subtle, classic prints (**2**) are another choice. Bolder designs (**3**) such as prints, plaids, and stripes add visual interest, but they may not coordinate with every garment you plan to wear with the completed jacket.

Outerwear lining. Special lining fabrics for warm winter coats are also available. Some are backed with special aluminum coatings (**1**); others are woven or laminated to a warm flannel backing (**2**). The color range in these specialized fabrics is usually limited. When a color match is impossible, interline a traditional lining fabric (page 111) with an insulating layer of fabric, such as lambswool (**3**) or flannel (**4**).

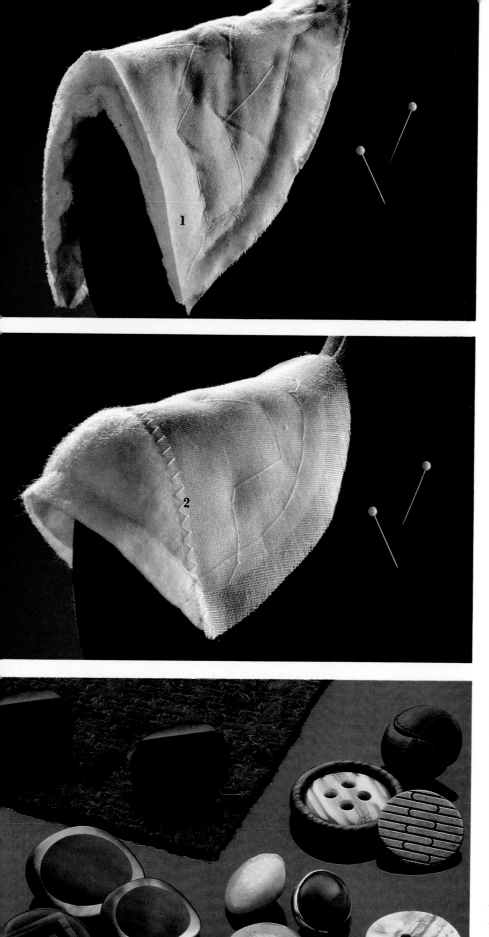

Special Notions for Tailoring

Shoulder pads play a key role in shaping tailored garments, and they are available in a variety of shapes and sizes. Standard shoulder pads **(1)** square the shoulders of garments with set-in sleeves. Use these for standard fit or extended shoulder styles. Raglan shoulder pads **(2)** softly support the shoulder area for a rounded shaping. They are used in garments that have raglan or dolman sleeves or dropped shoulders.

Shoulder pads should be large enough to cover the entire shoulder area, stopping about 1" (2.5 cm) from the neckline and extending in front to fill the hollow above the bust. In back, they should be narrow enough to clear the shoulder blades.

Check the pattern envelope for the correct pad thickness and style. Changing the thickness requires a change in fitting the shoulder area of the garment. Even when heavily padded shoulders are not a fashion trend, thin shoulder pads are used in tailored garments for soft shoulder shaping, support, and longer wear.

Special patterns for making your own shoulder pads are available, but to save time, you may want to use purchased shoulder pads. Choose covered styles for unlined or partially lined jackets and coats.

Buttons add distinction to a tailored garment and should suit the style of the garment. Simple, high-quality buttons, such as bone, horn, mother of pearl, and brass, work well on most tailored garments. Choose buttons with the garment fabric in hand, spacing them as they will be on the finished garment. Stand back to see how they will look from a distance. A larger or smaller button than the size specified on the pattern envelope may look out of proportion. Buy extra buttons for replacement purposes.

Pocketing fabric (1) is usually recommended for longer-wearing inner pockets in tailored garments, but is available only in basic colors. Substitute a lightweight firmly woven twill fabric **(2)** in cotton or a cotton/polyester blend if you are unable to find pocketing. Avoid stiff pocketings of 100 percent polyester. To reduce bulk, cut linings for patch pockets from lining fabric **(3)** rather than self-fabric.

Stay tape (shown twice the size) stabilizes seams to prevent stretching. At the lapel roll line, it also shapes the lapel to body curves. Taping shoulder seams shapes them to the curve of the shoulder. In custom tailoring, hair canvas seam allowances are removed, and stay tape secures the interfacing to the garment. Taping is optional with machine and fusible methods.

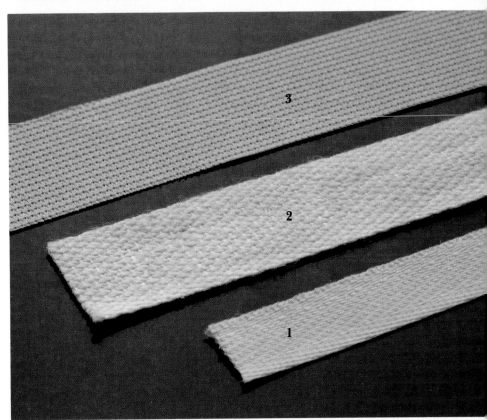

Ideally, stay tape is ⅜" (1 cm) wide, thin, and pliable, making it easy to control at corners and curves. Although polyester twill tape **(1)** is often used, plain weave tape **(2)** of cotton or linen is preferred; it is thin and shapes easily with steam pressing. It is not always available in fabric stores but can be purchased from a tailors' supply house. Warp knit stay tape **(3)** can be trimmed to ⅜" (1 cm), without raveling. Do not substitute seam binding; it is too wide and does not shape well.

Sleeve head (shown half the size) prevents the sleeve cap of a set-in sleeve from collapsing. Placed between the sleeve cap and the seam allowance, the sleeve head also prevents the seam allowance from showing through to the right side of the garment, and it gently shapes the sleeve. Purchase nonwoven sleeve heads **(1)**, or make custom sleeve heads **(2)** from bias strips of heavy flannel or lambswool (page 98).

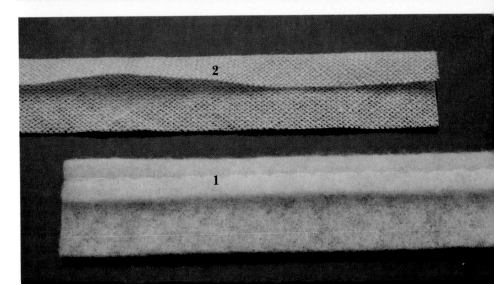

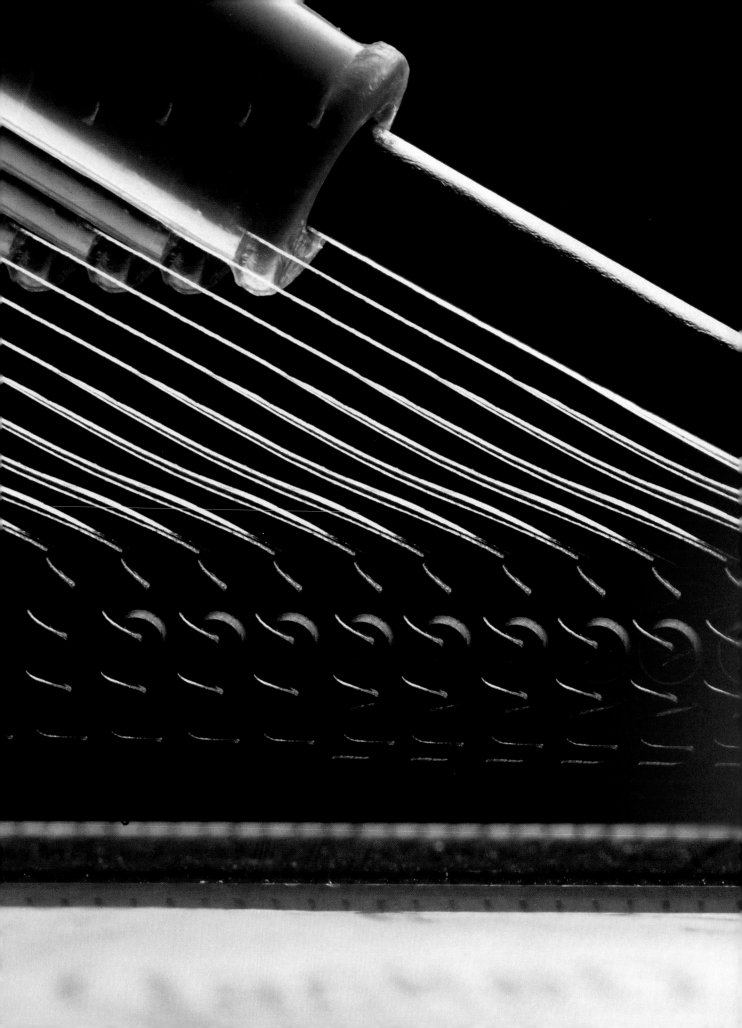

Tips & Tools

Cutting & Marking Tools

Selecting appropriate tools and using them correctly are important in tailoring. To produce high-quality garments, purchase the best tools that fit within your budget. Locate them in the notions area at a fabric store or in sewing mail-order catalogs. Tailors' supply houses in metropolitan areas are good sources for hard-to-find tailoring tools and notions. Check the Yellow Pages of the phone book under "tailors."

Accurate cutting and marking are essential for the garment to be assembled correctly and to fit well. Plan enough time to cut and mark all fabrics for the garment before storing the project. Moving and folding cut pieces, then marking later, is inaccurate because the pattern tissue shifts; folds in the tissue and fabric pieces result in distorted markings.

A large cutting surface makes cutting easier and more accurate, prevents fabrics from sliding and pulling out of shape, and doubles as a large pressing surface. To make your own cutting surface, pad a hollow-core door or a piece of pressed board or plywood that is at least 30" by 48" (76 by 122 cm). For the inner layers, use wool; for the outer surface, use heavy cotton muslin or canvas. Prewash the surface fabric to remove sizing, which scorches quickly, sticks to the iron, and soils your work. If possible, place the padded surface on a table or chest at a comfortable standing height. For a more permanent arrangement, pad the top of an inexpensive wooden table.

1) Bent-handled dressmaker's shears, below, with sharp, smooth blades are essential for cutting accuracy. The angle of the lower blade allows the fabric to lie flat as you cut. Buy the most comfortable length and size for your hand. Choose quality shears of hot-forged, high-grade, chrome-plated steel. An adjustable screw, not a rivet, joining the blades provides a smooth and comfortable cutting action. Oil the screw occasionally, and wipe lint from the blades frequently for the best cutting action.

2) Rotary cutter and mat **(2a)** can be substituted for dressmaker's shears if you are skilled and comfortable with these tools. Rotary cutters are available in two sizes: choose the large cutter for heavy coatings or thick, spongy fabrics; choose the smaller cutter for all other tailoring fabrics.

3) Tailor's points in a 5" (12.5 cm) length are double-pointed, very sharp scissors used for trimming, clipping, and snipping. In small and tight areas, these scissors give more control than long-handled shears. Careful, accurate trimming and clipping eliminate bulk and produce clean, sharp, flat edges, the mark of a carefully tailored jacket or coat. Duck-billed appliqué scissors **(3a)** may also be used for trimming seams.

4) Pinking shears are helpful for softening or feathering the edges of fusible interfacings. This technique ensures that interfacing edges will not be noticeable from the right side of the garment.

5) Long pins with large heads make it easier to pin into thick and spongy tailoring fabrics. Fine silk pins **(5a)** are ideal for silky lining fabrics.

6) Tailor's chalk and marking pens are readily available and easy to use. Clay chalk cakes in plastic containers with built-in sharpeners **(6a)**, powdered chalk in convenient dispensers **(6b)**, and chalk pencils **(6c)** work best on flat-surfaced fabrics. Waxed chalk cakes **(6d)** are better on textured wools and other nubby fabrics, but are difficult to remove on hard-surfaced fabrics. Pens with disappearing or water-soluble ink **(6e)** may leave marks on fabrics, especially if you press over the markings, so test first.

7) Tracing wheel, used with dressmaker's tracing paper **(7a)**, marks construction lines on lining and interfacing fabrics and smooth-surfaced, lightweight garment fabrics. The sawtooth wheel traces a distinct, thick line, suitable for most fabrics. Use a smooth-edged wheel on delicate surfaces.

8) Multi-strand embroidery floss makes quick work of tailor's tacks, eliminating the need to make and cut multiple thread loops. Darning cotton may also be used for this purpose.

9) See-through ruler with accurate ⅛" (3 mm) grid lines helps mark lines for padstitching on collar and lapels; it is also used in pattern alterations.

1

Trimming & Grading

Edges in tailored garments should be thin and crisp; seam edges should roll slightly to the inside. Achieve this by grading enclosed seam allowances. Trim seam layers in a staggered fashion, with the widest seam allowance lying against the garment to cushion the remaining seam layers so they do not show through to the right side. Seams that intersect are bulky. Eliminate as much thickness as possible by trimming at seam intersections.

To reduce the thickness of layers, trim sew-in interfacing close to the seamline. It is not necessary to trim fusible interfacings. When included in the seam allowance, they act as a stabilizer, making it possible to trim seams as close as ⅛" (3 mm) without fear of raveling. This is especially helpful in loosely woven fabrics and for curved enclosed seams.

Tips for Trimming and Grading Seams and Darts

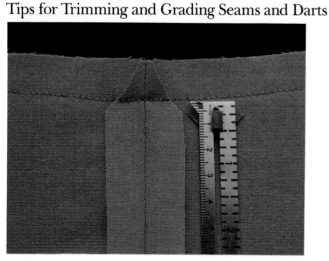

Trim seam allowances and darts on intersecting seams after pressing and before joining to the next section. Trim to ¼" (6 mm) below seamline.

Trim across collar and lapel points close to stitching. Trim diagonally along sides for a smooth, crisp point.

Grade enclosed seam allowances. Trim each layer a different width, with widest edge against garment. Firmly woven fabric may be trimmed to ⅛" (3 mm).

Grade neck facing seam allowances to ¼" (6 mm) to stagger the seam allowance layers. Do not trim garment seam allowances.

Notch outside curves close to stitching, removing wedges from seam allowance. Space notches closer together on deep curves, farther apart on shallow ones. Alternate notches on facing and garment.

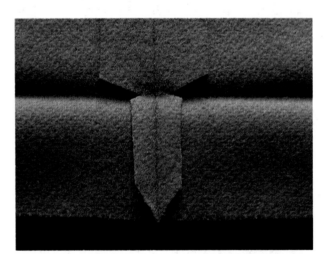

Notch seam allowances at hem foldline for thin, smooth fold, and trim seam in hem allowance to ¼" (6 mm). Trim diagonally at cut edge of hem to reduce bulk.

Bevel trimmed seams in thick fabrics to further reduce bulk after grading. Hold scissors at an angle, and skim trimmed edges.

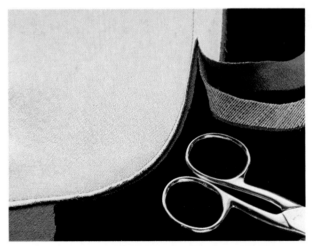

Shorten stitches around outside curves, and trim seam to a scant ⅛" (3 mm) in the curved area. Use this method when tailoring with fusible interfacings.

Pressing Equipment

Using the right pressing equipment with correct pressing techniques is essential to shaping a tailored garment to fit body contours smoothly. Pressing as you sew is as important as accurate stitching.

A press cloth of smooth fabric is a buffer between the iron and the garment fabric to prevent overheating, scorching, and surface shine. Use a dampened see-through press cloth for fusing. Wool press cloths hold moisture and protect the surface nap and texture in wools and synthetic suedes.

The best press cloth for pressing on the right side of fabric is often a large scrap of the garment fabric. Use a heavy press cloth to retain more moisture for pressing heavy fabric; use a lighter one for pressing thin, fine fabric. A cushioned pressing pad prevents flattening raised details, such as bound buttonholes, pockets, and flaps. Use a bristled press cloth or a velvetlike pad to avoid flattening napped or pile fabrics when pressing.

Cover the iron soleplate with a perforated iron guard for pressing on the right side of fabric without a press cloth. Remove the iron guard and clean the soleplate frequently to prevent corrosion from lint buildup and moisture.

1) Ironing press is suitable for tailoring with fusible interfacings. Fuse large garment sections in one step; or group and fuse small pieces, such as the collar and pocket pieces, on the bed of the press. Pressure of approximately 100 pounds (45.4 kg) ensures a good bond for interfacing when fused according to manufacturer's directions.

2) Professional ironing system with a gravity-flow steam system is expensive but worth the investment if you want to upgrade your equipment.

3) Steam iron provides heat and steam to shrink and shape fabrics. A large, heavy soleplate is necessary for fusing interfacings. Fusible interfacings require pressure from the weight of the iron for a smooth, permanent bond. An iron with a surge-of-steam button provides optimum steaming and eliminates the need for a dampened press cloth with a dry iron. For tailoring, avoid cordless and automatic-off irons, which do not maintain heat over a period of time. They make fusing time-consuming since you must wait for the iron to reheat periodically.

4) Tailor's pressing board is a small tabletop ironing board used for pressing details. The narrow end is the right size and shape for shrinking out sleeve cap fullness. Pressing boards and ironing boards should be padded with layers of wool to retain moisture. A soft, prewashed cotton cover absorbs excess moisture and helps prevent iron shine on garment fabrics. A padded cutting surface (page 31) is a good substitute for an ironing board. It provides support for the entire garment and eliminates stretching while the garment is damp with steam.

5) Tailor's ham is used for pressing shaped areas, such as darts, curved seams, collar, and sleeve caps. A wool covering on one side holds steam when you press wool fabrics. Use the cotton-covered side for pressing at high temperatures. A ham holder (**5a**) keeps the ham in the desired position and leaves your hands free to work with the garment and iron.

6) Pressing mitt is softly padded and fits over your hand or the end of a sleeve board. Use the mitt as a pressing surface in areas where a tailor's ham does not fit, especially shoulders and set-in sleeves.

7) Sleeve board is a miniature ironing board with two sides of different sizes for pressing small details and narrow openings, such as completed sleeve hems.

8) Clapper is a rounded wooden block used to flatten seams, folds, creases, and enclosed edges, such as facings and collars. Cool hardwood speeds steam removal and cooling to set the press.

9) Point presser is made of hardwood for pressing seams open in lapel and collar points. One type is attached to a clapper.

10) Seam roll is a firmly packed, tubular cushion for pressing all seams open without imprinting the seam edges to the outside of the garment. It is essential for pressing seams in completed sleeves. Narrow paper strips placed under dart and pleat edges also prevent edge impressions on the right side.

11) Contoured pressing board has numerous shaped, pointed, and curved edges and surfaces. Use without a pad for thin, crisp edges. Use with a pad for a softer edge finish and for details that should be shaped into the garment, such as set-in sleeves, darts, and shoulder and hipline seams.

12) Pointer and creaser is a flat wooden tool with a pointed end used to push out and turn sharp corners, and a rounded end used to crease and hold seams open for pressing.

Pressing Techniques

Careful step-by-step pressing, combined with trimming, clipping, and grading, eliminates excess fabric thickness and creates a crisp, custom finish. The goal is to produce seams, darts, edges, and corners that are smooth, flat, and thin. This cannot be achieved if all pressing is left until last or correct trimming, clipping, and grading methods are not used.

Correct pressing opens and flattens seams, hems, and enclosed edges without leaving imprints on the right side of the garment. It also sets the shape in curved seams and darts, and shrinks out fullness in sleeve caps and hems. The original texture, color, and finish of the fabric are retained when pressing is done correctly.

Tips for Pressing

Test iron setting and effects of steam on a sample seam and dart sewn in fabric scraps.

Press, using lower-pause-lift motion. Do not slide iron from place to place.

Press each seam before crossing another seam.

Do most pressing on wrong side of fabric. Use correct press cloth when pressing from the right side. The press cloth protects fabric from overpressing and from changes in fabric surface, hand, and appearance.

Do not press over pins or basting unless the basting is stitched with silk thread.

Keep seamline perfectly straight when pressing straight seams, so seams hang correctly. Press curved seams and darts on shaped pressing equipment to prevent distorted or stretched lines.

Allow pressed areas to cool before moving. If fabric must be moved, lift and support it with both hands to prevent the fabric from stretching out of shape.

Perfectly pressed

Perfectly pressed seams, darts, and edges are thin, smooth, and pucker-free with no edge imprints on the right side. Fabric texture does not change when pressed correctly.

Overpressed

Underpressed

Overpressed seams, darts, and edges imprint to the outside. Fabric is shiny and flattened from too much heat or pressure. Overpressing with too much moisture may shrink the seamline and cause ripples.

Underpressed edges are rounded, and seams and darts have pronounced wells, or indentations.

Two Ways to Use a Clapper

Steam a small section of seam at a time. Place clapper on steamed area, and press down, using both hands.

Hold clapper in place until area is cool and dry. Repeat, working in small sections for entire seam.

Steam and slap edges of enclosed seams and thick areas with clapper until smooth, flat, and crisp. For

thicker fabrics, increase pressure to light pounding with clapper; repeat, increasing pressure as needed.

How to Press an Enclosed Seam

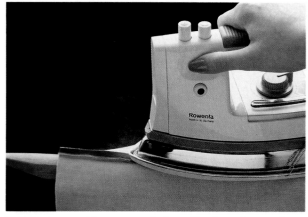

1) Press seam flat to set stitches. Grade, trim, and notch or clip seam allowances (pages 32 and 33). Press open on point presser. Use contoured pressing board for curved seams.

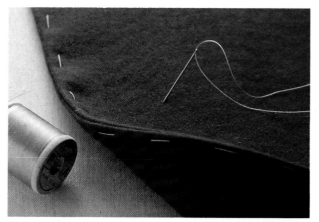

2) Turn right side out. Roll finished edge to underside or inside; baste near edge with silk thread. Press, using clapper as above. Dry thoroughly; remove basting.

How to Press a Plain Straight Seam

1) Press seam flat to blend stitches into the fabric, eliminate puckers, and smooth the stitching line.

2) Place seam over seam roll; keep it perfectly straight. Open and gently crease seam, using fingers or blunt end of point turner. Penetrate seam with steam; glide point of iron along seamline groove.

3) Use clapper to force steam into the fabric, especially in hard-to-press fabrics.

4) Press on right side with iron guard or press cloth to protect fabric from direct iron contact. Press with grain, using entire sole of iron in up-and-down, not sliding, motion.

How to Press a Curved Seam

1) Notch outside curves to remove excess fabric (page 33). Make notches or clips close and deep enough so seam allowances lie flat and smooth. Clip inside curves so they lie flat. Press flat.

2) Position seam on similarly shaped contour of tailor's ham or contoured pressing board; press. Press seam from right side as in step 4, above.

Pressing & Shaping Darts

Darts create contours and curves in a flat piece of fabric. Proper pressing using a tailor's ham or contoured pressing board maintains the stitched-in shape. Unless pattern directions indicate otherwise, press vertical darts toward the center front or center back; press horizontal darts downward.

How to Press a Dart

1) Press dart along stitches from wide end to within ⅜" (1 cm) of point. Do not press beyond point. Use clapper, if necessary, to press a sharp, flat crease at edge of dart.

2) Place dart smoothly over tailor's ham, with edge of dart facing as it will be in finished garment. Tuck paper strip under edge of dart to avoid overpressing. Press across dart from wide end to ⅜" (1 cm) from point.

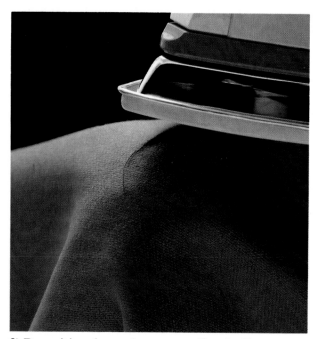

3) Reposition dart point over small end of ham, and press gently to shrink and ease point into garment.

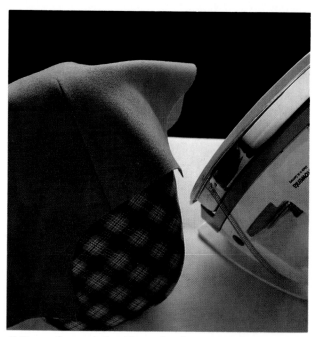

4) Press from right side, using iron guard or press cloth; press from wide end to point. Reposition to press dart point. Allow to dry thoroughly to set shape.

Three Alternative Ways to Press Darts

Wide dart. Trim dart to ½" (1.3 cm); do not trim point. Press along stitching; do not crease point. Press open; press point to one side or into box pleat. For easier pressing, insert knitting needle. Press from right side as in step 4, opposite.

Double-pointed dart. Clip once or twice at widest part of dart to within ⅛" (3 mm) of stitching. Follow steps 1 to 4, opposite, pressing half the dart at a time from center to point.

Dart in lightweight fabric. Press along stitching; do not crease edge. Place on ham, with paper strips under edges; press dart flat. Stop ½" (1.3 cm) from point. Reposition on ham to shape point. Press from right side as in step 4, opposite.

Tips for Correcting Pressing Errors

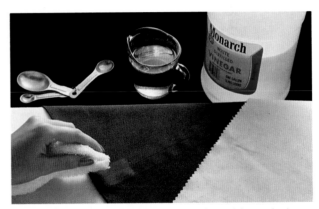

Remove basting thread marks by using several thicknesses of damp press cloth on fabric. Hold iron over press cloth, supporting weight of iron with hand.

Remove shine from fabric by sponging with a solution of 1 to 2 teaspoons of white vinegar to 1 cup of water. (Test first on fabric scrap for colorfastness.) Cover area with a press cloth; press lightly.

Remove edge imprints on right side of fabric by placing iron point under seam or hem edge; steam press gently. Place paper strip under edge; press.

Remove needle holes from ripped-out stitches by steaming heavily, then brushing with a soft clothes brush or toothbrush.

Raise flattened nap by steaming, then brushing the surface with a soft clothes brush.

Tools & Stitches for Handwork

Custom-tailored garments require more handwork than most other garments. Use the appropriate tools, and master the special hand stitches to hold fabric layers in place or to build in shaping.

Special hand stitches hold interfacing and fabric layers together and secure edges of stay tape, hems, and facings. Fasten a single strand of thread with two or three small stitches. Stitches must be tight enough to hold the layers securely but loose enough to prevent the stitches from pulling, puckering, and breaking from wearing strain.

Tools for Handwork

Needles for custom tailoring are short and fine to make short, invisible stitches. Buy a package of betweens (tailor's needles) in assorted sizes 5 to 10 (45 to 70).

Thimble is a must to protect the index finger while hand stitching. It should have a comfortably snug fit.

Tweezers are handy for removing tailor's tacks and basting threads.

Silk thread is very fine and smooth and does not leave stitch impressions from pressing. Use for basting areas before pressing and for all permanent hand stitching. If silk thread is unavailable, use a high-quality, long-staple polyester thread. Use silk thread for hand sewing only, because it will require continuous adjustments on the top and bobbin tension for machine sewing.

Beeswax coats and strengthens hand-sewing thread and reduces tangling and knotting. Stitches stay in place better when the thread is waxed. Draw thread across the cake of beeswax; press the waxed thread with a hot iron to melt the wax into the thread and to remove excess wax. Pressing softens the thread, making it easier to handle. Use unwaxed thread for temporary basting.

Hand Stitches for Tailoring

Padstitching in custom-tailored garments holds the interfacing in place, and it adds body and shaping. To build in shape, make small, permanent, invisible stitches while holding fabric in wearing position.

Featherstitching decoratively secures back pleats in linings. Substitute machine stitching if desired.

Slipstitching invisibly joins the folded edge of the lining hem or finished edges of pockets and welts to the garment.

Tailor basting holds large areas of interfacing in place and controls fabric layers. Large, diagonal stitches may be temporary or permanent.

Fellstitching holds stay tape securely in place to stabilize edges. Straight machine stitching may be substituted to save time.

Bar tacking reinforces points of strain, such as pocket corners. Very short, narrow machine zigzagging may be substituted for bar tacking.

Catchstitching invisibly secures interfacing edges to the garment.

Tailor's hemstitching invisibly weaves the hem allowance to the garment. For a more secure stitch in heavy fabrics, use catchstitching.

Uneven basting is for general basting and for marking construction and placement lines. Permanent uneven basting holds interfacing in hemline folds.

Speed tailor's tacks are used for marking fabrics. If desired, use different thread colors for different symbols. Use darning cotton or six-strand embroidery floss. Multiple strands of embroidery floss grab into the fabric, do not pull out easily, and require a single stitch. Use continuous speed tailor's tacks on lapel roll lines, foldlines, and pocket placement lines.

Tips for Padstitching

Short stitches in closely spaced rows create a crisp, sharply tailored garment. Longer, more widely spaced stitches create a softer look.

Stitch length should be the same as distance between stitching rows. For example, if padstitches are ¼" (6 mm) long, distance between the rows of stitches should be ¼" (6 mm).

Short, fine needle should be used with single strand of waxed silk thread that closely matches garment fabric.

Padstitching rows run parallel to roll line in fall of undercollar. Padstitching in stand may run perpendicular if a crisper roll line is desired. Padstitching in lapels runs parallel to roll line.

Fabric is rolled as you stitch; the tighter you roll the fabric, the more roll that is created in the layers. Roll tighter close to the roll line, less toward the outer edge until you reach the collar or lapel point. Increase the curve slightly in the points, so finished collar and lapels will roll slightly toward the garment.

How to Padstitch

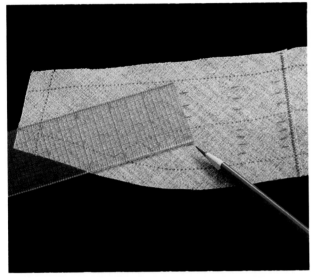

1) Mark padstitching lines on hair canvas interfacing, using a soft lead pencil and see-through ruler. Do not extend stitching lines into seam allowances.

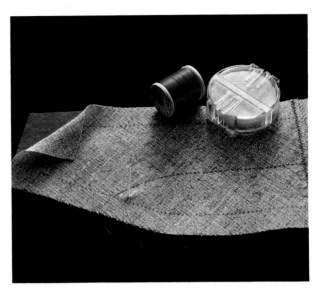

2) Place interfacing on wrong side of garment piece; baste. Stitch in place two or three times to secure waxed thread to interfacing at end of stitching line closest to collar or lapel roll line.

3) Roll fabric layers over index finger, and take a short stitch perpendicular to the stitching line through the interfacing, catching only a thread of the garment. Interfacing may shift slightly.

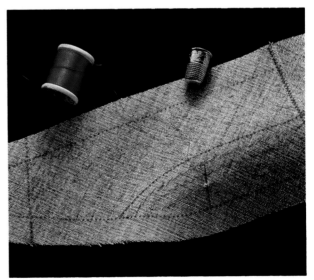

4) Stitch ¼" to ½" (6 mm to 1.3 cm) from first stitch, and continue to end of row; do not pull stitches tight. Move needle to next stitching line and continue, creating rows of chevron stitches.

Hand Stitches for Tailoring

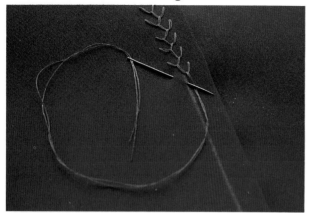

Featherstitching. Take each stitch diagonally across marked guideline, holding thread under needle point. Tug slightly on stitch to make it taut but loose enough that thread curves slightly. Alternate direction of stitch from one side of guideline to the other.

Slipstitching. Secure single strand of waxed thread through folded edge. Take tiny stitch in garment, catching only a thread or two. Slip needle into fold again for ¼" (6 mm), then out to take next stitch in garment.

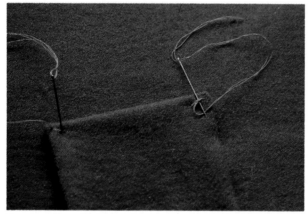

Bar tacking. Take two or three long stitches in the same place. Working left to right, cover with closely spaced blanket stitches; insert needle under bar tack and over thread loop. Pull loop tight.

Catchstitching. Work left to right, taking stitches with needle pointing left. Catch a thread or two of garment above interfacing edge. Take next stitch in interfacing edge ¼" to ⅜" (6 mm to 1 cm) to the right. Space evenly; do not pull tight.

How to Make Speed Tailor's Tacks

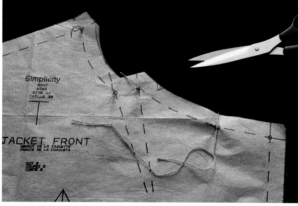

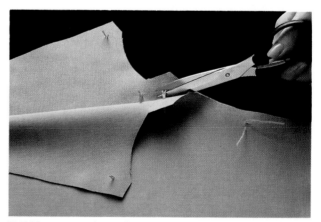

1) Use long length of six-strand embroidery floss or darning cotton. Take stitch through construction mark, leaving 1" (2.5 cm) tail at beginning and end.

2) Lift pattern from fabric carefully. Separate fabric layers no more than ½" (1.3 cm). Clip threads between, leaving thread tufts on each layer of fabric.

Tailor basting. Take horizontal stitches from right to left and parallel to one another to make long, diagonal floats between. For permanent tailor basting, catch only a thread of garment fabric in each horizontal stitch.

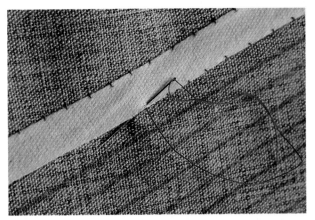

Fellstitching. Work right to left; take short, closely spaced stitches perpendicular to, and just through edge of, stay tape and interfacing. Catch a thread or two of garment fabric.

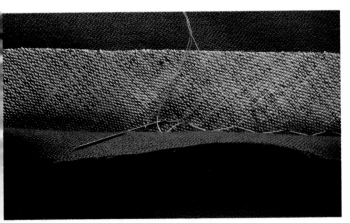

Tailor's hemstitching. Fold hem allowance back. Take small horizontal stitch in garment, catching only a thread or two. Take next stitch ¼" (6 mm) to the left in hem allowance. Space evenly.

Uneven basting. Take short stitches ½" to 1" (1.3 to 2.5 cm) apart for temporary work. For permanent stitching in hemlines, catch only a thread or two of the garment fabric, spacing stitches ⅜" to ½" (1 to 1.3 cm) apart.

How to Make Continuous Speed Tailor's Tacks

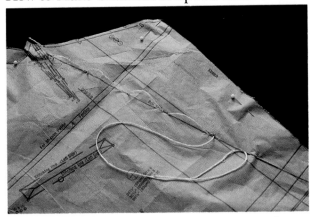

1) Take first stitch, leaving 1" (2.5 cm) tail. Continue taking small stitches every 2" (5 cm), leaving slack between stitches.

2) Snip slack thread. Lift pattern from fabric. Separate fabric layers no more than ½" (1.3 cm). Clip threads between stitches, leaving tufts on each layer of fabric.

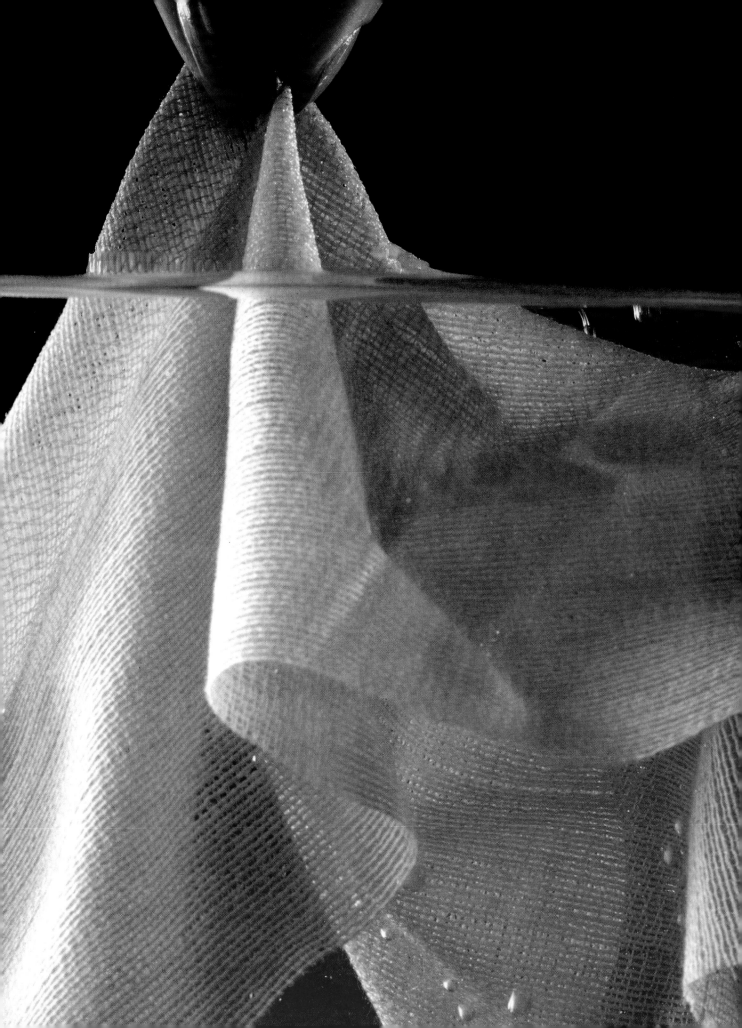

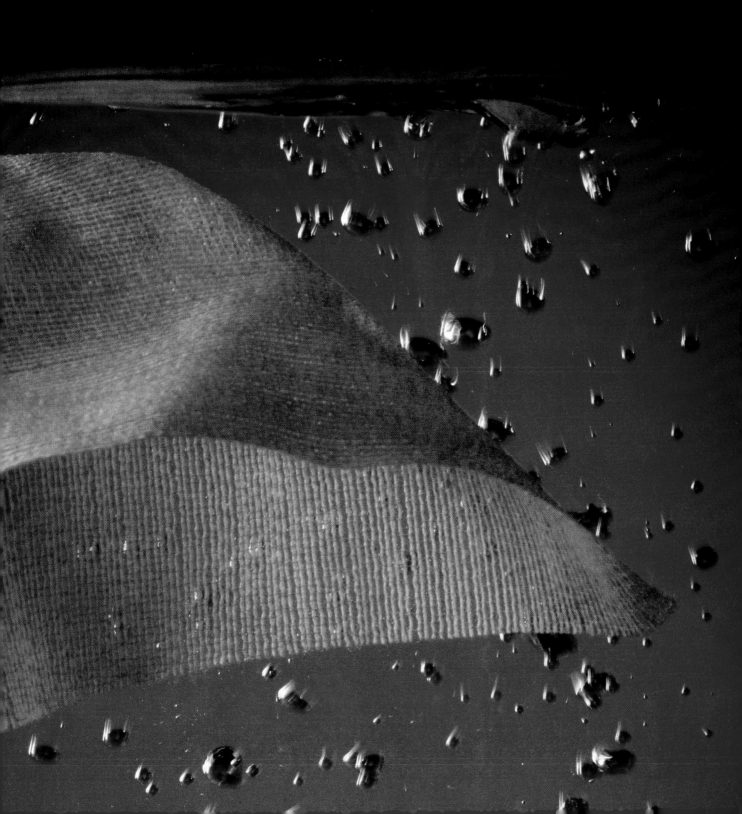

Getting a Good Fit

Selecting the correct pattern size is important in tailoring. Fit is most critical through the shoulders and neckline. To prevent extensive pattern changes in these areas, choose the pattern size according to the bust or high bust measurement. Check the pattern catalog for how to measure and determine the correct pattern size.

Pin-fitting the pattern before cutting the fabric gives you an idea of how the finished garment will fit and suggests pattern adjustments to make. Making a test garment (pages 50 to 53) after pin-fitting is recommended for accurate fit and design corrections. Major adjustments to accommodate a full bust, swayback, and full upper arms should be made on the test garment. They cannot be made after the garment is cut from the garment fabric. If you decide not to make a test garment, cut wider seam allowances in the garment body to allow for construction fitting.

Before pin-fitting and making the test garment, evaluate the ease in your pattern. Jackets and coats require *wearing ease* to fit comfortably over other garments. Refer to the wearing ease chart, below. Unlined jackets and close-fitting styles may require less ease; coats to be worn over heavy sweaters require maximum ease. There may also be extra *design ease* in the pattern to create a current fashion look. If you want your garment to look the way it does on the pattern envelope, maintain this design ease.

Measure the pattern, and compare the measurements with your body measurements. Make the adjustments necessary for the right length and the correct size to fit around bustline, waistline, hipline, and upper arm. Include enough wearing ease and design ease to achieve the desired fit and fashion look.

Guidelines for Jacket and Coat Wearing Ease

Fitting Area	Amount of Ease
Bustline	3½" to 6" (9 to 15 cm)
Hipline	3½" to 6" (9 to 15 cm)
Upper arm	3" to 5½" (7.5 to 14 cm)
Upper back	1½" to 3" (3.8 to 7.5 cm)

How to Pin-fit a Pattern

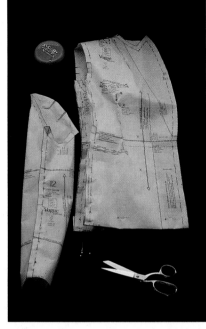

1) Pin hems and darts or tucks in place. Pin main pattern pieces, wrong sides together; place pins on seamlines, with points toward hem. Mark front and back waistline. Lap and pin sleeve seamlines, but do not pin sleeve to pattern body.

2) Try on pattern with shoulder pads in place; wear clothing that will be worn with completed garment. Pin pattern to shoulder at neckline of blouse or dress. Check fit in front of full-length mirror.

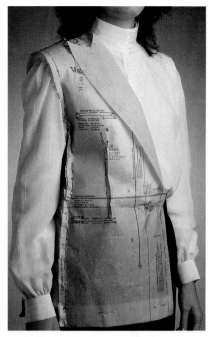

3) Check fit in bustline, waistline, hipline, and area across upper back. Adjust pins in side seams and center back for a comfortable fit. Darts should stop ½" to 1" (1.3 to 2.5 cm) from bust point if vertical, slightly farther away if horizontal. Adjust garment length.

4) Check lapel for smooth fit. If lapel gapes or breaks at roll line more than ½" (1.3 cm), make an adjustment for gaping lapel (page 53). For gapes less than ½" (1.3 cm), tape the roll line (pages 70 and 72).

5) Check to make sure side seams hang straight and perpendicular to the floor, and back vent hangs straight without spreading open. If not, make an adjustment for swayback (page 53).

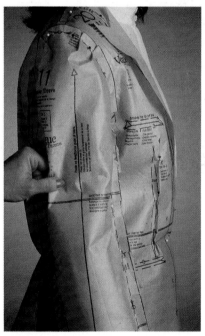

6) Slip arm into sleeve; pinch out fullness across upper arm. Pinch should be at least 1½" (3.8 cm) deep for ease in jacket sleeve or at least 2" (5 cm) for coat sleeve. Check the sleeve length.

Making a Test Garment

Making a test garment, often called a *muslin*, is highly recommended. The more fitted the style, the more important it is to test the fit first. Making a test garment allows you to check pattern adjustments, perfect the fit before cutting the garment fabric, and test desired style changes. If the lapel and undercollar roll lines are not marked on the pattern tissue, you can establish and mark them on the test garment and then transfer them to the pattern.

The test garment can be made from any inexpensive, firmly woven fabric in a weight similar to the garment fabric. This gives an accurate reading of how the garment will fit and hang. Making a test garment takes a few extra hours, but cutting and constructing it carefully and accurately is worth the effort even though the test garment will never be worn.

After pin-fitting the pattern and making necessary adjustments, cut the jacket front, back, sleeves, and undercollar from the test fabric. Allow 1" (2.5 cm) seam allowances on the shoulders and all lengthwise seams. Mark placement lines, including roll lines, and construction symbols on the right side of the fabric. Also mark the center front, waistline, hemline, sleeve cap crosswise grain, and lengthwise grain on the right side.

Stitch the test garment, and try it on over garments similar to the ones to be worn with the finished jacket or coat. Refer to the fitting guidelines, opposite. Work from shoulder to hemline. Make adjustments affecting width and length before correcting other areas. Eliminate any wrinkles pointing to problem areas, making sure grainlines hang straight. Minor fitting adjustments require simple seamline changes. Major changes require tucking to eliminate excess fabric or slashing to add fabric for full body curves. These changes must be perfected in the test garment.

When fitting the test garment, make it slightly larger than the fit of the final garment. This allows for the thickness of the garment fabric and the extra room taken up by the lining and interfacing layers. Mark all changes on the pattern before cutting the garment fabric. Make corresponding changes on facing, interfacing, and lining pieces.

How to Make a Test Garment

1) Staystitch neck seamline. Machine-baste test garment, and press seams open. Turn, press, and pin hem. Stitch undercollar to neckline; turn and press undercollar and lapel seam allowances. Complete sleeves; set into armholes, using machine basting.

2) Try on test garment with shoulder pads in place; pin at buttonhole locations with center fronts matching. Release seams 2" (5 cm) above waistline, if necessary, to let out waist and hip. Check darts and garment length. Correct additional fitting problems.

3) Adjust sleeve length over bent arm. Finished edge should extend ½" to 1" (1.3 to 2.5 cm) over wristbone. Thick fabrics need maximum amount; sleeves shorten as wearing creases develop.

Guidelines for Fitting Jackets and Coats

Vertical seams hang straight and perpendicular to floor.

Fronts hang straight at the hemline without spreading open.

Bustline darts point to, and stop short of, fullest part of bust.

Shoulder seams lie on top of shoulders and appear straight, without pulling toward the front or back.

Set-in sleeves are smooth and pucker-free with softly rounded caps. There are no diagonal wrinkles in sleeve cap, and sleeve does not pull across upper arm.

Sleeves cover wristbone by ½" to 1" (1.3 to 2.5 cm).

Collar hugs back neckline without gaping or wrinkling across the back.

Lapels hug the bustline without gaping when garment is buttoned.

Back vent hangs straight and perpendicular to floor without spreading open across seat.

Hem is straight and parallel to floor at a fashionable and flattering length. Hemline does not hike up in front or back.

Garment fits around body smoothly without pulls or wrinkles. Reaching does not cause strain across upper back.

Garment is comfortable over clothing intended to be worn with it.

4) Determine roll lines if pattern is not marked. Pin fold on one lapel and on undercollar to center back.

5) Press roll line to create a crease. Remove stitching from garment front and undercollar. Place garment pieces on pattern pieces, matching markings. Transfer roll lines to pattern pieces.

6) Cut welt or patch pocket template from stiff paper; do not include seam allowances. Check pocket size, shape, and position; adjust as desired. Mark new position.

Adjustment for Forward Shoulder Thrust

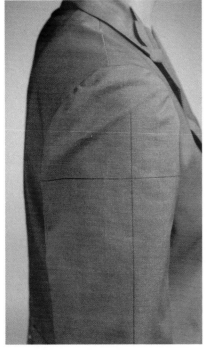

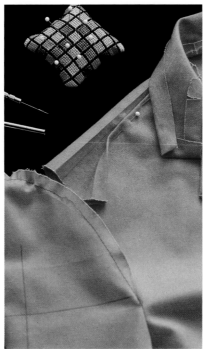

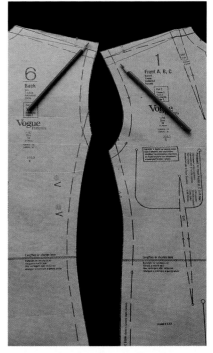

Poor fit makes shoulder seam pull toward back at top of arm. There are wrinkles across back neck, curving to shoulder seam. Sleeves bind uncomfortably.

1) Release back shoulder seam allowance; take in front shoulder seam allowance at armhole, tapering to neckline. Move shoulder dot to match adjustment, as in step 2, below.

2) Measure the change in test garment, and transfer to pattern, extending back shoulder and shortening front shoulder. Blend new cutting lines into original lines.

Adjustment for Sleeve Wrinkles

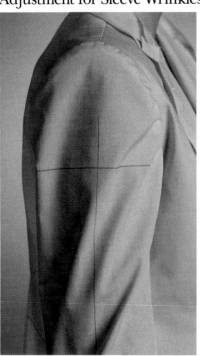

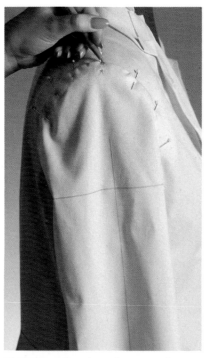

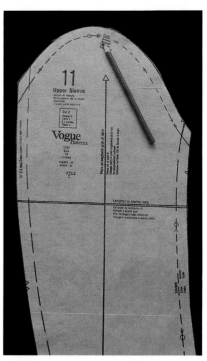

Poor fit creates diagonal wrinkles in either front or back of sleeve because of shape and curve of upper arm and back.

1) Release basting above notches, and rotate sleeve in armhole toward front or back to eliminate wrinkles. Redistribute ease. Mark the new shoulder dot position on sleeve.

2) Transfer new shoulder dot position to sleeve pattern piece. Make same change on the lining pattern piece.

Adjustment for Gaping Lapel

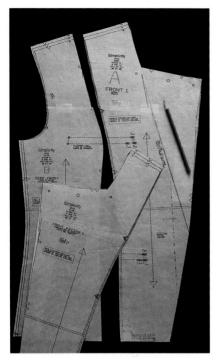

Poor fit makes the lapel gape or break, even though bustline fits correctly and hemline is parallel to the floor.

1) Shorten the lapel. Make a tuck in garment front, across lapel, tapering to armhole.

2) Make same change in jacket front, facing, lining, and interfacing pattern pieces. Straighten the lapel roll line.

Adjustment for Swayback

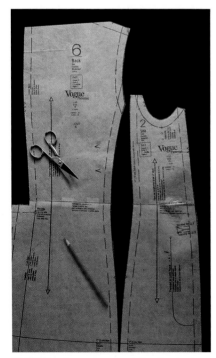

Poor fit causes side seams to swing forward and back vent to spread open.

1) Take a tuck in jacket at center back above vent so the vent and side seams hang straight and perpendicular to floor. Taper tuck to side seams.

2) Make the same tuck in the jacket back and lining pattern pieces. Straighten grainline.

Preparing the Pattern

In addition to fitting adjustments, patterns for tailored garments often require style changes and alterations in the pattern pieces before cutting. You may prefer pockets, flaps, and back vents featured in other patterns. Welt pockets can be substituted for patch pockets. It is also possible to add a lining or partial lining to an unlined jacket pattern. After pin-fitting the pattern or making the test garment, adjust pattern pieces if necessary. Make corresponding changes on all pattern pieces affected by the changes, including facings, interfacings, and lining pieces.

Four Pattern Adjustments for Professional Results

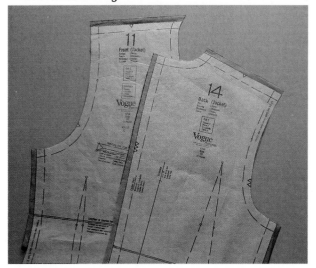

Cut 1" (2.5 cm) seam allowances at shoulder, side, and center back. When a test garment is not made, wider seam allowances are essential for fitting during construction. Wider seam allowances in unlined jackets are easier to handle for seam finishes.

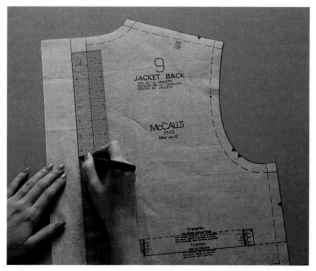

Add a center back seam allowance to one-piece jacket or coat patterns. This provides an additional fitting seam and creates the illusion of a slimmer torso.

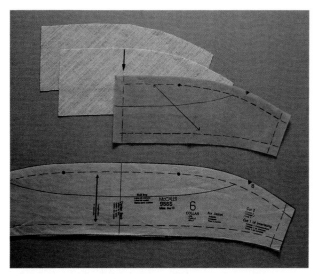

Change a one-piece undercollar to a two-piece undercollar by adding a ⅝" (1.5 cm) center back seam (arrow); cut on bias. Both collar points must be cut on same bias grain for uniform shape, shading, and design. Cut undercollar interfacing the same way.

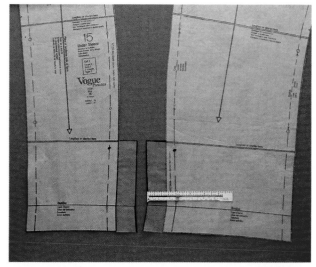

Add a vent to a two-piece sleeve. Draw new cutting line on upper and under sleeve 2" (5 cm) from and parallel to back sleeve seamline. Extend foldline for hem; draw new cutting line for top of vent 4½" (11.5 cm) from hem. Mark dot on seamline ⅝" (1.5 cm) from top of vent for end of stitching.

Pattern Adjustments for Interfacing

Not all patterns include pieces for the interfacing shapes that tailors use to provide better shaping and support at the armhole, neckline, front, and back. When pattern pieces are provided, they may not cover a large enough area and necessary seam allowances may be eliminated. Use the pattern pieces for front, side, and back to make interfacing patterns from tissue paper, tracing paper, or lightweight nonwoven interfacing.

When using sew-in interfacing such as hair canvas, partially interface the front of a jacket or coat to give the desired shaping without unnecessary stiffness.

When using fusible interfacing, partially or completely interface the front of a jacket or coat, depending on fabric drape and garment style. Fusible interfacings that are fused to the entire jacket front give added body to lightweight fabrics, but may be too firm for softer jacket styles. Select fusible interfacings according to the guidelines on pages 20 to 22.

Add a front shoulder reinforcement to ensure a smooth line from shoulder to bustline and to prevent the area from collapsing. Cut reinforcement on the true bias from hair canvas, firmly woven interfacing or muslin, or fusible weft-insertion interfacing. Use a loftier fabric, such as lambswool, to fill in distinct hollows between the shoulder line and upper curve of the bustline on small-busted figures.

Add a back stay of firmly woven interfacing to stabilize the garment and prevent stretch across the shoulders and armholes; do not use fusible interfacing. A back stay also supports the garment shape while on a hanger.

Raglan sleeves require a stay in the neck and shoulder area to provide a foundation for shoulder pads and to prevent shoulder pads from showing through light-colored fabrics. The raglan sleeve stay bridges the gap between the back stay and front interfacing; it keeps the neckline shape, drape, and appearance uniform from front to back.

For stability and longer wear, interface hems in sleeves and the lower edge of the garment. Use hair canvas or fusible interfacing, and extend the interfacing past the hemline fold to cushion the edge (page 101).

Two Ways to Cut Interfacing for a Jacket Front

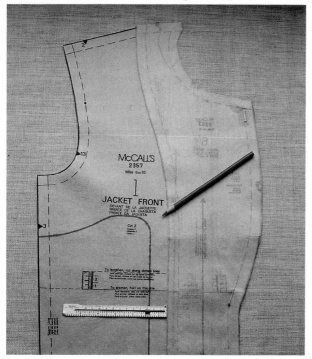

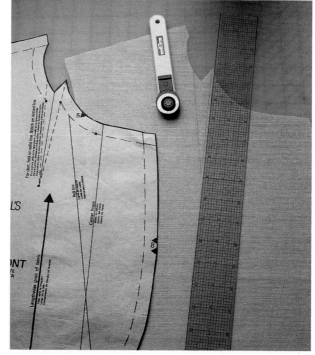

Sew-in interfacing. Draw new interfacing shape on jacket front 1" (2.5 cm) wider than facing pattern piece. Curve cutting line above bustline for full bust, or 1" (2.5 cm) below it for small bust. Extend to side seam 3" (7.5 cm) below underarm. (For styles with side panel, cut interfacing as two pieces.)

Fusible interfacing. Cut entire front from fusible interfacing; cut out darts on stitching lines before fusing. Or cut fusible interfacing as for sew-in interfacing, left, with inner edge along dart stitching line; pink inner edge.

How to Cut Interfacing for a Back Stay

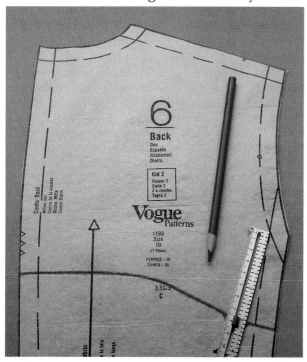

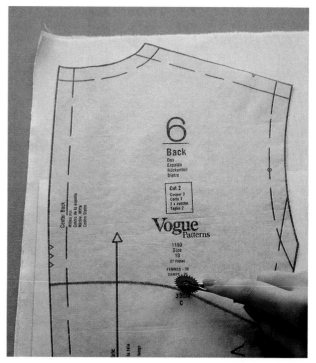

1) Draw line on jacket back pattern piece that curves from a point 8" to 10" (20.5 to 25.5 cm) below neckline to a point 3" (7.5 cm) below underarm.

2) Trace shape onto muslin or firmly woven interfacing. Cut on straight grain.

Two Ways to Cut Interfacing for a Shoulder Reinforcement

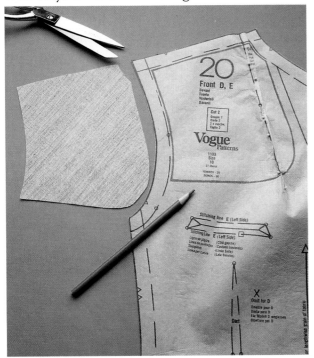

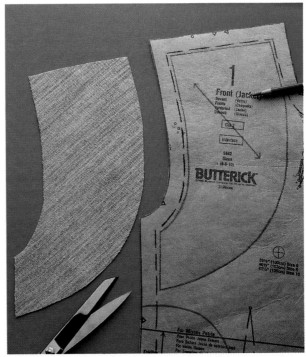

Standard jacket. Draw shape on front pattern ⅛" (3 mm) inside shoulder and armhole seamlines, stopping two-thirds of the way down the armhole. Draw line across to ½" (1.3 cm) from roll line, then parallel to roll line. Cut interfacing on bias grain.

Close-fitting jacket. Draw shape on front pattern ⅛" (3 mm) inside shoulder and armhole seamlines. Extend shoulder reinforcement into underarm for more support. Cut ½" (1.3 cm) shorter than front interfacing at underarm. Curve cutting line above bustline, then parallel to roll line. Cut interfacing on bias grain.

How to Cut and Attach a Raglan Sleeve Stay

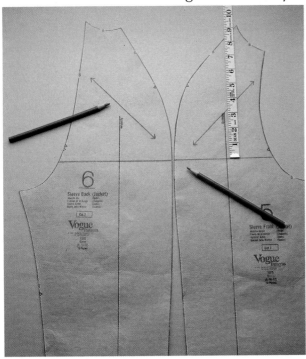

1) Draw a line 8" to 10" (20.5 to 25.5 cm) below neckline on raglan sleeve pattern pieces. Mark bias grainline.

2) Cut stay from muslin or firmly woven interfacing; pink lower edge. Before constructing sleeves, baste to wrong side of raglan sleeves at seamline edges.

Preparing the Lining Pattern

Lined jackets are easier to slide on and off than unlined ones, and they have a finished look on the inside. Linings also hide the interior construction, such as interfacings and shoulder pads.

If you like the styling of an unlined jacket pattern but prefer to sew a lined jacket, it is easy to make your own lining pattern. Extra ease may be added to the lining pieces to reduce strain on the lining seams.

For loose-fitting jackets, another choice is to make a partial lining, which covers shoulder pads and interfacings. A partially lined jacket is cooler to wear than a fully lined one. In partial linings, the front facing extends to the armhole to cover the front interfacing and meets the shaped back lining. The jacket back pattern is used to make the pattern for the lining, and the back neck facing is eliminated. A back pleat or back stay is not necessary. The curved edge of the back lining allows freedom of movement.

Even when a jacket pattern includes lining pieces, tailoring professionals recommend a few pattern changes. Add extra room to the sleeve lining pattern in the underarm area, so the lining will cover garment seam allowances without binding and pulling.

Adjust the lining pattern to match fitting adjustments in the garment. If you do not plan to make a test garment, cut the lining seam allowances for the shoulders and lengthwise seams 1" (2.5 cm) wide to allow for fitting changes. Cut the sleeve and garment lining the same length as the garment pattern pieces, trimming any excess when completing the hems.

A back pleat extends the wear of the lining, keeping sleeves from tearing under stress. Although some lining patterns do not include a back pleat, it is a simple pattern change to make.

How to Prepare a Lining Pattern

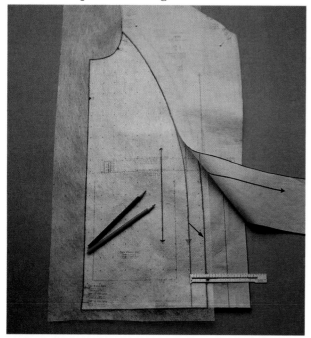

1) Cover jacket front pattern with tracing paper or tissue; place front facing pattern on top, matching markings. On tracing paper, draw outline of facing. Draw cutting lines for lining; inner curve cutting line (arrow) should be 1¼" (3.2 cm) from facing line to allow for ⅝" (1.5 cm) seam allowance. Mark grainline.

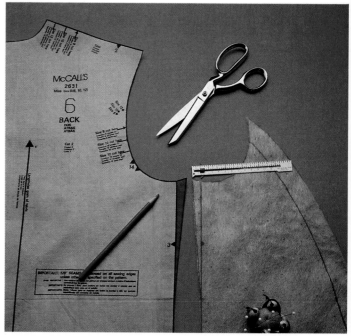

2) Add ½" (1.3 cm) to front and back side seam allowances at underarm area of lining, tapering to waistline. [If jacket has side panels, add ¼" (6 mm) to each seam allowance of side panels, front, and back.] This extra amount will be eased in when lining sleeve is attached.

How to Cut a Partial Lining for an Unlined Jacket Pattern

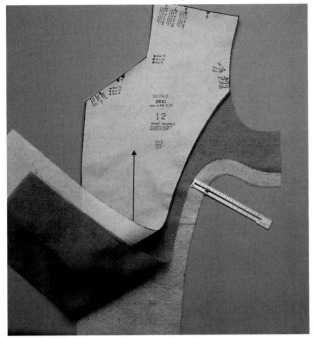

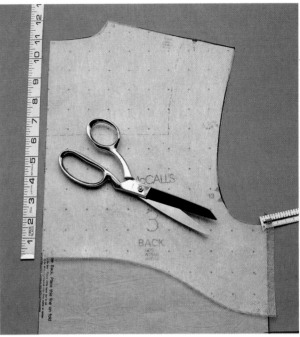

1) Place facing pattern on shaped front interfacing (page 56), matching notches. On tracing paper, trace around outer edges of pattern. Draw new cutting line for inner curve 1" (2.5 cm) beyond interfacing edge. Mark grainline. Use as pattern to cut partial lining from garment fabric.

2) Place tracing paper on back pattern piece. Draw back lining shape on tracing paper, curving from 10" to 12" (25.5 to 30.5 cm) below center back neckline to match width of front facing at underarm. Add ¼" (6 mm) to side seam for ease. Mark new grainline. Cut from lining fabric. Cut sleeve lining as in step 4, below.

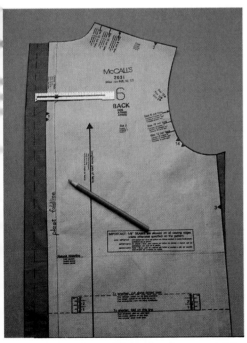

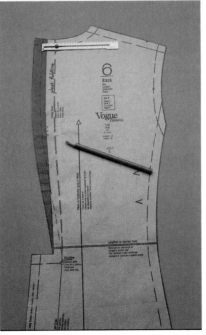

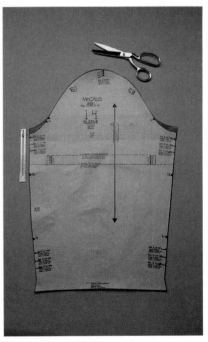

3a) Jacket without back vent. Add 1" to 1½" (2.5 to 3.8 cm) for back pleat at center back seam. Mark new seamline and pleat foldline.

3b) Jacket with back vent. Add 1" to 1½" (2.5 to 3.8 cm) for back pleat, tapering to top of vent. Mark new seamline and pleat foldline.

4) Cut sleeve lining, using garment pattern piece. Add ⅝" (1.5 cm) at underarm of sleeve, tapering to notches. Cut lining the same length as jacket sleeve pattern.

Preparing the Fabric

Examine, straighten, and preshrink tailoring fabrics before cutting. First, carefully examine the garment and lining fabrics for minor flaws and color variations. Mark flaws, such as yarn slubs or loose yarn ends, with basting. Avoid the flaws during pattern layout, or place the pattern so the flaw is in an inconspicuous location, such as a hem or seam allowance.

Straighten the crosswise ends of the fabric by tearing, pulling a thread, or cutting along a woven design line in the fabric. Then check the grainline by placing the straightened fabric on a table with selvages matching along one edge of the table. If the grain is straight, the fold is smooth and flat; the straightened edges also line up perfectly, with the crosswise grain perpendicular to the table edge. If the grain is not straight, stretch the fabric on the true bias. If stretching does not correct the problem, choose a different fabric that can be straightened. Garments that are cut off-grain will not hang correctly, and seams may twist out of line, affecting the fit and appearance.

Preshrink garment fabrics and linings after straightening. Refer to the care instructions for the fabric to determine the correct preshrinking method. Although some fabrics are labeled "needle-ready," it is a good idea to preshrink them anyway. In general, preshrinking loosely woven fabrics and those made of natural fibers is especially critical because they are more likely to shrink when you press them than tightly woven fabrics and those made of synthetics or synthetic blends.

If you plan to use fusible interfacings, preshrinking the garment fabric is particularly important. Because fusing requires more steam pressing than normal, the garment fabric is likely to shrink during fusing.

Have a drycleaner thoroughly steam press garment fabrics marked "dryclean only." It is not necessary to dryclean, too, unless there is noticeable soil. Be sure to ask the drycleaner to avoid pressing a crease. If you have a large cutting surface and an iron with a surge of steam, you may do the steam pressing yourself, being careful not to miss any areas. Steam press with the grain, never on the bias. Allow steamed fabric to dry thoroughly before working with it. If yardage is longer than the pressing surface, press section-by-section and allow to dry before moving.

Preshrink washable fabrics used for stays and woven sew-in interfacings in the same way that you will care for the finished garment. Also, preshrink fusible interfacings. Although some bolts are marked "preshrunk," it is wise to preshrink fusible interfacings of the knit, woven, or weft-insertion types in hot water, opposite. Or steam shrink knit or nonwoven fusible interfacings, opposite. Do not preshrink fusibles in the washer and dryer because the adhesive resin may dissolve in the washer or fuse in the dryer.

How to Preshrink Stay or Edge Tape

Immerse cotton or linen stay or edge tape in hot water. Roll in towel to remove excess moisture, and allow to air dry completely. Press when dry if needed. Pressing while damp causes stretching and distortion.

How to Preshrink Hair Canvas

Mist hair canvas with spray bottle, and press dry. Or roll in a damp towel just removed from the washer. Allow hair canvas to absorb moisture from the towel for several hours or overnight; then press dry.

How to Preshrink Fusible Interfacing (immersion method)

1) Fill sink or bathtub with hot water. Gently fold fusible interfacing into water. Soak until water is cool. Drain water, and allow interfacing to sit for 5 minutes.

2) Remove interfacing carefully; roll in towel to remove excess moisture. Drape over towel bar or shower rod, and allow to dry.

How to Preshrink and Apply Fusible Interfacing (steam-shrink method)

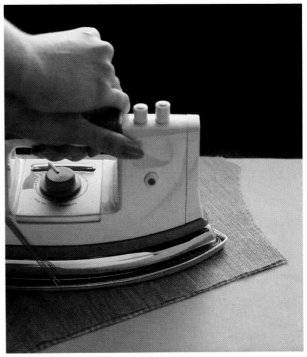

1) Place interfacing, resin side down, on garment fabric. Hold steam iron just above interfacing, and steam gently for a few seconds. Interfacing edges draw up slightly as you steam, but slight difference in size does not affect finished product.

2) Use iron soleplate guard or press cloth; fuse, following manufacturer's directions. On large pieces, work from center toward edges.

Tailoring Techniques

Constructing the Jacket

Once the pattern and fabric are prepared, carefully cut and mark the jacket, and you are ready to sew. Standard ⅝" (1.5 cm) seam allowances have been used in the pages that follow; however, when cutting the fabric, you may want to add 1" (2.5 cm) seam allowances to the shoulder and vertical seams. This gives extra room for fitting adjustments, and 1" (2.5 cm) seams are easier to press than ⅝" (1.5 cm) seams. For partially lined jackets, 1" (2.5 cm) seam allowances are also easier to finish.

Choose the desired method of tailoring (pages 12 and 13), and cut the interfacing pieces (pages 55 to 57). Mark the garment pieces at all construction notches, dots, and placement lines, including roll lines. Tailor's tacks (pages 44 and 45) are the marking method preferred by most tailors.

Instructions for tailoring a traditional notched-collar jacket are included because it has the greatest amount of tailoring detail. The variations for tailoring a shawl-collar jacket are on pages 84 and 85. For other styles, such as collarless jackets, ignore the instructions that do not apply. Shaping the body of the jacket will be the same except in the collar and lapel areas. The pattern guidesheet will give instructions for jackets with special design details.

The sequence for tailoring a jacket or coat is given in the chart below. Even if you have never tried tailoring before, some of the steps will be familiar to you from your previous sewing experiences.

Sequence for Tailoring a Jacket

Shape the undercollar.

Apply fusible interfacing, if used, shaping and constructing jacket front.

Attach pockets, if included.

Sew bound buttonholes, if included.

Apply hair canvas interfacing, if used, shaping and constructing jacket front.

Attach back stay.

Shape shoulder seams. For a fitting, side seams or side panel seams may be basted or permanently stitched at this time.

Attach raglan sleeves, if included.

Tailor notched or shawl collar, if included.

Stitch side seams or side panel seams.

Attach set-in sleeves, if included.

Insert shoulder pads.

Tailor hems and vents.

Insert lining or partial lining.

Sew machine buttonholes, if included.

Sew on buttons or covered snaps.

Shaping the Undercollar

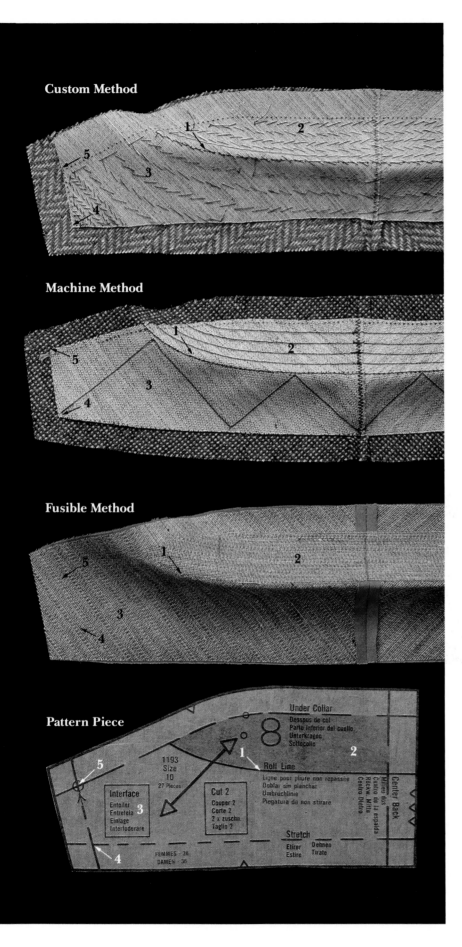

Custom Method

Machine Method

Fusible Method

Pattern Piece

The undercollar is interfaced to add body and shape. The interfaced undercollar supports the weight of the upper collar.

The roll line **(1)** is the dividing line between the two areas of the undercollar, the stand **(2)** and the fall **(3)**. The stand is shaped so it hugs the back of the neck and holds the collar to the correct height in back. The fall is shaped to curve gently, with the collar points **(4)** rolling slightly toward the garment. The place where the collar and lapel meet is commonly called the collar notch **(5)** and should not be confused with the construction notches on the pattern tissue.

Consider the fabric and the available time when selecting the custom, machine, or fusible method for tailoring. Any one of the three methods will give good results. Because the undercollar is a small piece to handle, it is a good choice for testing a tailoring method.

Hair canvas is the interfacing choice for both the custom tailoring and machine tailoring methods. If the custom method is used, hand padstitching shapes the undercollar; if the machine method is used, padstitching is done using machine stitches. After padstitching, the undercollar is positioned over a tailor's ham and steamed to set the shape.

For the fusible tailoring method, select a fusible interfacing that is appropriate for the fabric and style of the garment. The fusible method uses steam shaping instead of padstitching.

How to Shape the Undercollar (custom method)

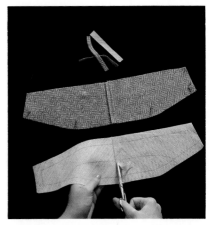

1) Cut and mark undercollar and hair canvas. Stitch undercollar seam; trim to ¼" (6 mm), and press. Lap seamlines in hair canvas. Zigzag stitch; trim close to stitching.

2) Mark lines on hair canvas for padstitching. Mark ¼" (6 mm) apart in stand and ⅜" (1 cm) in fall; near collar point, space lines closer. Or use alternative marking below.

3) Pin hair canvas to undercollar, wrong sides together; hand-baste on roll line between seam allowances.

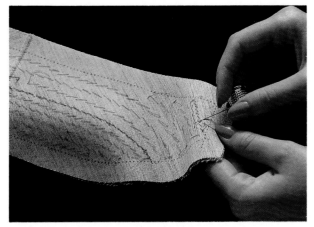
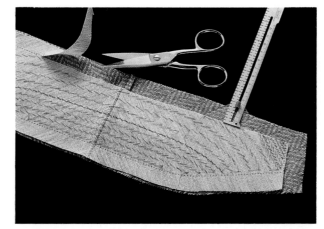

4) Padstitch interfacing to collar as in steps 3 and 4, page 43. Padstitch roll line, stand, and fall. Stitch back and forth, stopping ⅛" (3 mm) from seamlines.

5) Trim the hair canvas just beyond seamlines on the outer edges of undercollar so hair canvas is not caught in seams. Do not cut into the padstitches.

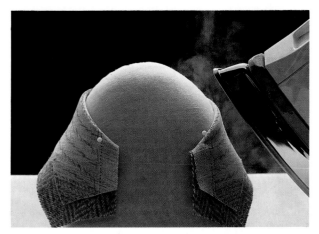
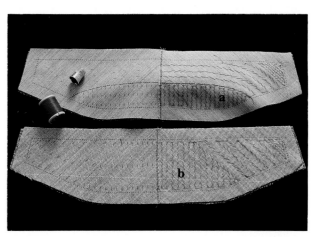

6) Fold the undercollar on roll line. Pin to tailor's ham. Steam to set the shape; do not press a crease at roll line. Dry undercollar thoroughly before moving.

Alternative marking. For crisp look **(a)**, mark lines perpendicular to roll line in the stand. For collar to be worn up in back **(b)**, eliminate roll line and mark lines parallel to center back; mark remaining area as shown.

How to Shape the Undercollar (machine method)

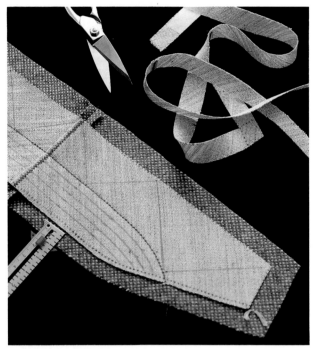

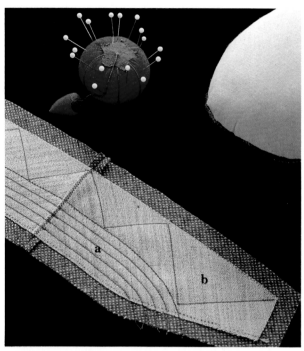

1) Mark padstitching lines in stand, step 2, opposite. Mark remaining area, following grainline as shown. Trim hair canvas ½" (1.3 cm) from raw edge on neckline; trim remaining edges on seamline. Machine-stitch hair canvas to undercollar on roll line.

2) Machine-stitch stand **(a)** on padstitching lines, working from center back to seamline. Stitch fall of collar **(b)**, starting at center back and following marked lines. Shape undercollar, step 6, opposite.

How to Shape the Undercollar (fusible method)

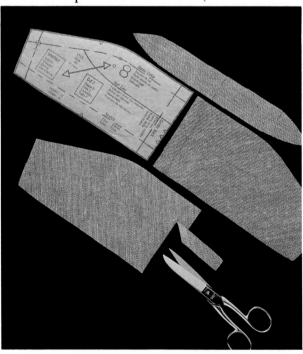

1) Cut undercollar from fusible interfacing; transfer markings to right side. Trim off seam allowance at center back. Cut strip of interfacing the size and shape of stand so crosswise grain goes around neckline; do not include seam allowances.

2) Fuse interfacing to undercollar. Stitch center back seam; trim to ¼" (6 mm), and press open. Fuse interfacing strip to stand. Shape the undercollar, step 6, opposite.

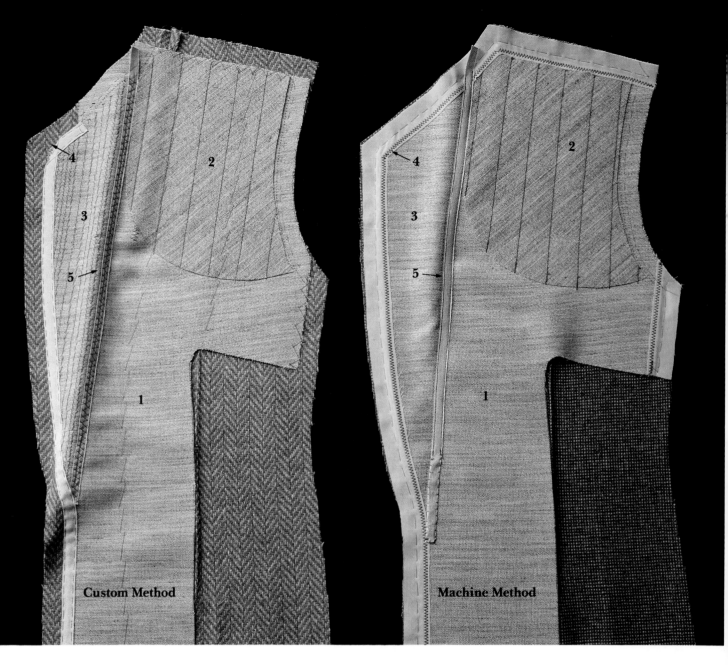

Custom Method

Machine Method

Shaping the Jacket Front

Interfacing the garment front builds shape into the jacket or coat and contributes to the long-lasting good looks of the garment. Choose either the custom, machine, or fusible method. The pattern piece is used for cutting the interfacing and shoulder reinforcement and for marking the roll line.

Front interfacing (1) helps the garment front to drape smoothly over the body; garment front edges hang straight, and pockets are supported. The shoulder reinforcement (2) ensures a smooth line from shoulder to bustline.

Because the garment front piece turns back to form the lapel (3), pay special attention to shaping this area. The completed lapel should roll back smoothly and curve slightly inward at the lapel points (4). Tape the lapel roll line (5) with stay tape by hand or machine so the lapel lies close to the body without gaping. This step is especially important for a full-busted figure.

When using the custom method, tape the front edges with stay tape to stabilize them. This step is optional in machine or fusible methods, but may be helpful for loosely woven fabrics.

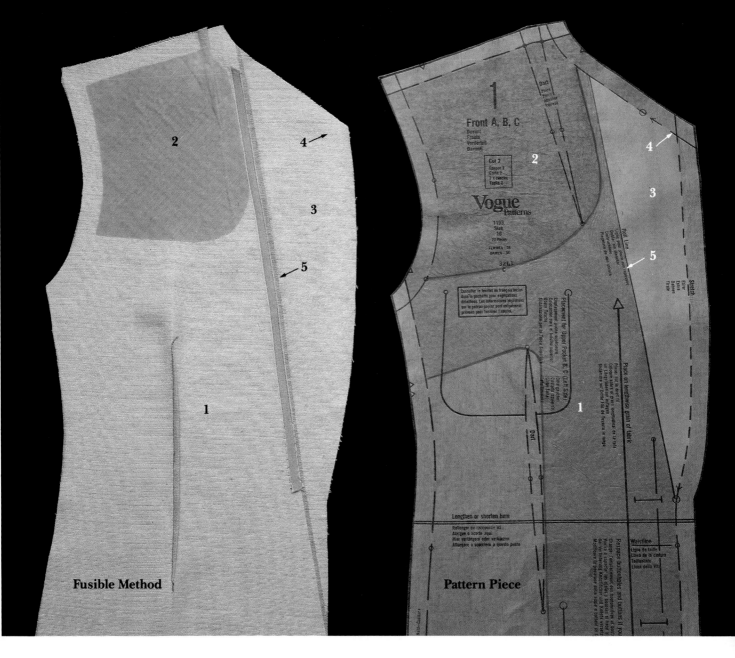

Fusible Method

Pattern Piece

How to Shape the Jacket Front (custom method)

1) Cut front interfacing from hair canvas (page 56). Transfer darts, seamlines, and roll line. Cut the shoulder reinforcement (page 56) from hair canvas or lambswool.

2) Mark padstitching lines to seamlines. Place one line on each side of roll line (arrow) ⅛" (3 mm) away; then space lines ¼" (6 mm) apart. Near the lapel point, space lines closer.

3) Cut out wedge of hair canvas on dart stitching lines. Position on tailor's ham, bringing dart edges together. Place 1" (2.5 cm) strip of lightweight fusible interfacing over dart; fuse. Zigzag cut edges together.

(Continued on next page)

4) Trim side and shoulder seam allowances to ⅛" (3 mm) beyond seamlines so hair canvas is not caught in seams. To support set-in sleeve, hair canvas is not trimmed in armhole seam.

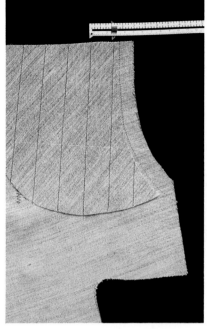

5) Mark lines 1" (2.5 cm) apart on shoulder reinforcement if using woven interfacing. On marked lines, machine-baste to front interfacing.

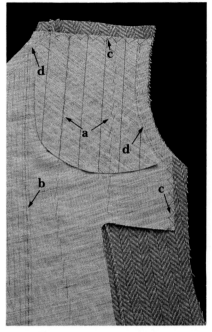

6) Tailor-baste (a) interfacing to jacket front, matching collar notches and roll lines. Baste **(b)** to roll line through all layers; catchstitch **(c)** to garment at side and shoulder seams. Baste **(d)** to armhole and neckline ½" (1.3 cm) from raw edges.

7) Cut ⅜" (1 cm) stay tape the length of roll line. Position ⅛" (3 mm) from roll line. Pin end of tape at lower end of roll line. Mark neck seamline on tape; pull tape so mark is ¼" to ½" (6 mm to 1.3 cm) into seam allowance; pin.

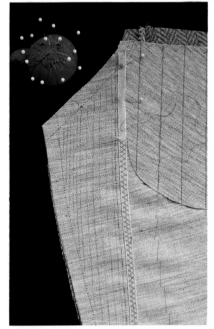

8) Pin remainder of tape in place, easing garment to tape in bust area. Catchstitch tape, catching a thread of garment in each stitch, or fellstitch along both edges.

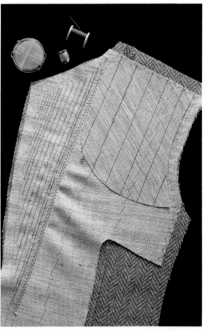

9) Padstitch (page 43), rolling lapel over finger. On roll line and next line, make stitches ⅛" (3 mm) long; then make stitches ¼" (6 mm) long. Near lapel point, roll more tightly and shorten stitches. Stop ⅛" (3 mm) from seamline.

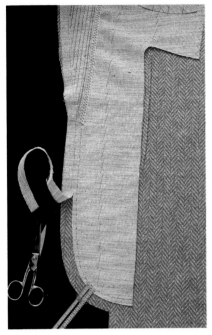

10) Attach hair canvas to garment from lower end of roll line to lower edge of garment, using permanent uneven basting 1" (2.5 cm) from raw edge. Between lower edge and collar notch, trim hair canvas ¾" (2 cm) from garment raw edge.

11) Measure garment front from collar notch to lower edge. Cut piece of ⅜" (1 cm) stay tape to fit. For curved lapel and curved lower edge, shape tape to fit, using pattern piece as guide.

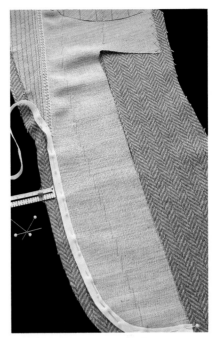

12) Pin tape with one edge *next* to ⅝" (1.5 cm) seamline and covering edge of hair canvas. Begin at lower edge, and work to roll line. At the roll line, turn lapel back against the jacket front to allow ease in tape for the lapel to roll.

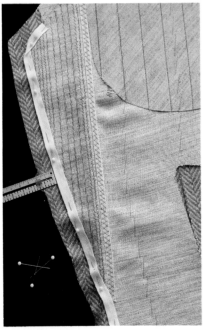

13) Pin tape on outer edge of lapel, folding tape back on itself at lapel point. Continue pinning around outer edge to collar notch. Repeat for other front; compare fronts for equal length and ease at roll line. Adjust if necessary.

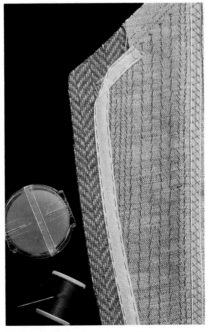

14) Attach both edges of tape to garment with permanent uneven basting or fellstitching.

15) Roll a damp hand towel into a flat pad ½" (1.3 cm) thick. Tuck pad under lapel. Steam the roll line without pressing a crease. Allow to dry overnight to set lapel.

How to Shape the Jacket Front (machine method)

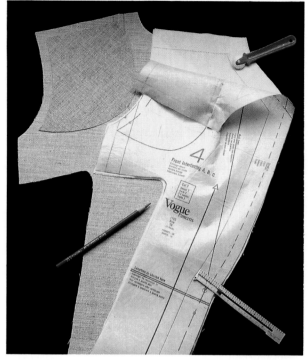

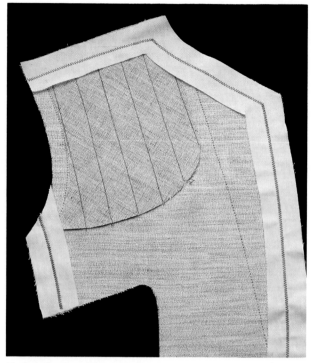

1) Cut front interfacing and shoulder reinforcement from hair canvas (page 56). Draw cutting lines for carrier strips 1½" (3.8 cm) in from outer edge of interfacing pattern at side, shoulder, neckline, and front. Transfer shape to muslin; cut carrier strips.

2) Apply shoulder reinforcement, step 5, page 70. Position carrier strips on interfacing, and stitch ¾" (2 cm) from raw edges with zigzag stitching or two rows of straight stitching. Trim outer edge of hair canvas close to stitching.

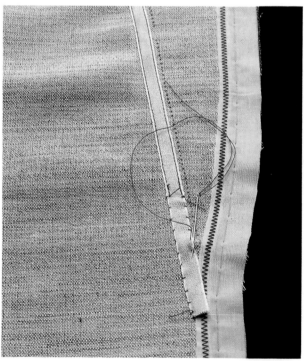

3) Trim inner edges of carrier strips close to stitching. Baste to garment ½" (1.3 cm) from edge.

4) Cut and pin stay tape as in steps 7 and 8, page 70. Machine-stitch both edges of tape through all layers. End stitching 2" (5 cm) from lower end of roll line; fellstitch or catchstitch remaining tape so stitches do not show on right side.

How to Shape the Jacket Front (fusible method)

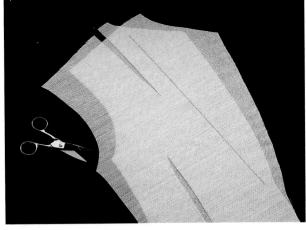

1) Cut front interfacing from fusible interfacing (page 56). Cut out wedge of interfacing on dart stitching lines.

2a) Crisp roll line. Cut interfacing on roll line. Trim ⅛" (3 mm) along the roll line from larger section. Position and fuse both sections to garment front.

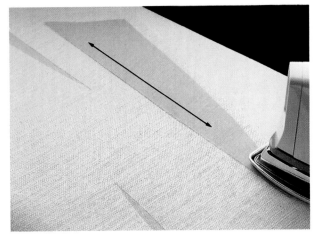

2b) Soft roll line. Cut extra lapel section of interfacing to fit from roll line to seamlines. Place the roll line on straight grain of interfacing to stabilize. Position and fuse interfacing with two layers in lapel area.

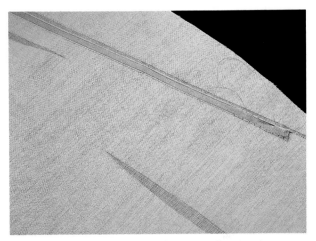

3) Determine whether roll line requires taping, step 4, page 49. Tape roll line as in step 4, opposite.

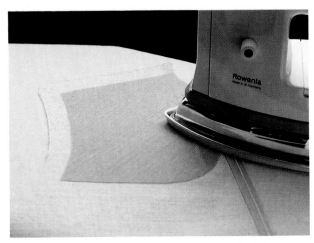

4) Cut the shoulder reinforcement from fusible interfacing (page 56). Position and fuse reinforcement to front interfacing.

5) Roll a damp hand towel into a flat pad ½" (1.3 cm) thick. Tuck pad under lapel. Steam the roll line without pressing a crease. Allow to dry overnight to set lapel.

Shaping the Jacket Back

To stabilize the shoulder area of a jacket or coat, a back stay is applied. A back stay also prevents strain in the garment fabric across the shoulder blades and supports the fabric to create a smooth line.

The back stay is cut from a firmly woven interfacing, cotton broadcloth, or muslin. The seam allowances of the back stay are caught in the seamlines during construction, eliminating the need for stabilizing the back neckline with tape. The exception is a collarless garment, which is subjected to more wearing strain and should be taped at the back neckline.

More fullness is needed to fit the back shoulder because of its rounded shape, so ease is built into the back shoulder seam allowance. Care must be taken in stitching and pressing to preserve this subtle shaping in a tailored garment. Tape the shoulder seams to shape the garment to your body and to keep the seams from stretching. Shaped shoulder seams may appear curved after they are stitched and pressed, but they will not appear curved when you wear the garment.

How to Make a Back Stay

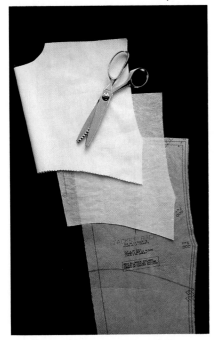

1) Cut back stay, steps 1 and 2, page 57. Overlap and stitch any seams and darts, step 1, page 66. Pink the lower edge.

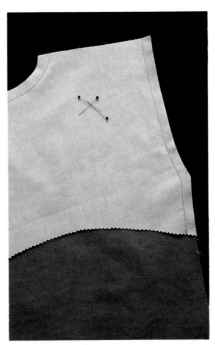

2) Prepare garment back, stitching and pressing seams, darts, and vents. Position back stay on garment; baste neckline, armhole, and side.

Collarless jacket. Tape back neckline by placing edge of stay tape ½" (1.3 cm) from raw edge at back neck. Clip tape so it lies flat. With fellstitching, catch edges of tape to back stay only.

How to Shape the Shoulder Seam

1) Pin shoulder seams, right sides together; ease back. Cut stay tape the length of front seamline. Mark tape ¼" (6 mm) from one end; for rounded shoulders, mark ⅜" (1 cm) from end.

2) Pin tape to front shoulder seam, with mark at raw edge. Center tape over seamline, and ease seam evenly. Stitch seam over tape. Backstitch at ends of seam.

3) Trim back stay close to stitching. Press seam over tailor's ham, curving seam toward the front.

Tailoring a Notched Collar

Most patterns do not include interfacing in the upper collar and facing. Adding a lightweight fusible interfacing to these two areas stabilizes the garment fabric and makes it more compatible with the layers in the garment front and undercollar. Joining the upper collar/facing unit to the undercollar/garment unit is easier because the layers are similar in weight and texture, and seams do not slip when stitched. The extra layer in the lapel and upper collar also acts as a buffer to help obscure enclosed seam edges.

Choose either fusible knit or lightweight weft-insertion interfacing to keep weight and thickness to a minimum. Test both on a scrap of garment fabric, and choose

the most compatible. Include the interfacing in the seam allowances on mediumweight fabrics. The fusible interfacing helps set the press in enclosed seams. If your garment fabric is heavy, trim ½" (1.3 cm) from interfacing seam allowances before fusing.

If using fusible knit interfacing, cut interfacing for garment front and upper collar on lengthwise grain. If using weft-insertion interfacing, cut front interfacing on the lengthwise grain, and the upper collar on the true bias so it curves gently around the neckline. If the garment has a back neck facing, do not interface this piece.

How to Prepare the Collar and Facing

1) Cut interfacing for upper collar and front facing, following grainline directions, opposite. Fuse and allow to cool.

2) Stitch back neck facing, if included, to front facing. Press seams open; trim to ¼" (6 mm). Staystitch facing on neckline edge. Clip facing to staystitching at collar notches (large dots).

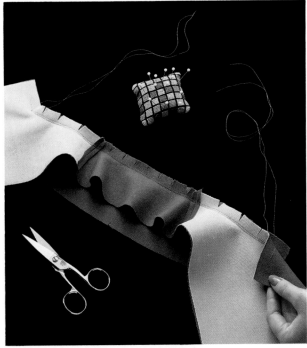

3) Pin upper collar to facings between collar notches, right sides together. Match center backs and shoulders; clip facings to staystitching as needed. Stitch from collar notch to collar notch; do not catch upper collar seam allowances in stitching. Stitch back and forth to secure ends, leaving 10" (25 cm) thread tails at collar notches.

3a) Garment without back neck facing. Stitch front facings to upper collar only. Begin at collar notch, and end at shoulder mark on upper collar; do not catch upper collar seam allowances in stitching. Stitch back and forth to secure ends, leaving 10" (25 cm) thread tails at collar notches.

(Continued on next page)

How to Prepare the Collar and Facing (continued)

4) Pin undercollar to garment; match markings and roll line. Clip garment to fit undercollar. Stitch from collar notch to collar notch (arrows); do not catch undercollar seam allowances in stitching. Stitch back and forth to secure ends, leaving 10" (25 cm) thread tails at collar notches. Clip to collar notches.

5) Compare lapels on upper collar/facing unit and lapels on undercollar/garment unit; pin together at collar notches. If lapels are not the same size or collars do not match, release stitching to shoulder and re-stitch neckline seams.

How to Trim and Press Neckline Seams

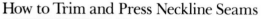

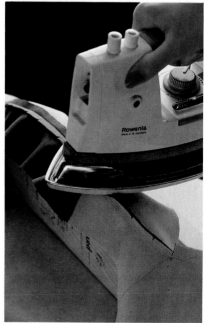

1) Trim neckline seam allowances of upper collar/facing unit to ⅜" (1 cm). Press open on contoured pressing board; use clapper.

2) Trim neckline seam allowances of undercollar/garment unit to ¼" (6 mm). Trim back stay close to neckline stitching. Trim hair canvas in undercollar and neckline seam allowances of garment front.

3) Press seam open on contoured pressing board; use clapper. Catchstitch neckline seam allowances to hair canvas interfacing to within 2" (5 cm) of collar notch on undercollar/garment unit.

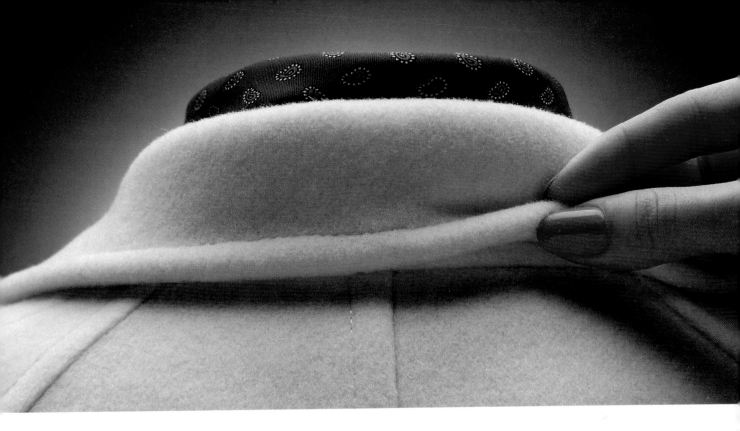

Adjusting for the Turn of the Cloth

Whenever two or more layers of fabric are held together in a curved position, the upper layer must be slightly larger than the under layer to allow for the curve, or the *turn of the cloth*. In a tailored jacket, the upper collar must be larger to go up and over the roll of the undercollar. The completed collar should cover the neckline seam in back, as pictured above, without rolling out at the edge.

Although most patterns are cut with extra ease in the upper collar and lapel edges for the turn of the cloth,

the thickness and weight of the garment fabric may require more than the pattern allows. Before stitching the upper collar/facing unit to the undercollar/garment unit, adjust for the turn of the cloth in the upper collar from shoulder to shoulder across the back. Then attach the upper collar/facing unit to the undercollar/garment unit, and complete the collar, carefully following the directions on pages 80 to 83. The collar and lapel will have a flat, smooth collar notch without tight puckers and pulls.

How to Adjust the Collar for the Turn of the Cloth

1) Pin neckline seams of upper collar and undercollar, with wrong sides together and shoulder seams matching. Place pins in seamline. Position on dress form or shaped hanger.

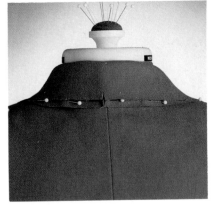

2) Mark position of upper collar raw edge on undercollar, using pins. If collar edges match, this marking is not necessary.

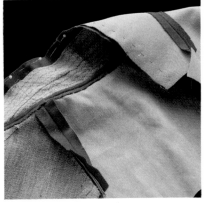

3) Pin collars, right sides together, matching raw edge of upper collar to pins on undercollar. Hand-baste from undercollar side on 5/8" (1.5 cm) seamline.

1) Draw accurate seamlines on lapels of garment. Start at last stitch of neckline seam, and draw to lapel point, then 1" (2.5 cm) down side.

2) Pin small tucks about ½" (1.3 cm) inside seamlines at points of upper collar and facing. This causes seam edge to roll to underside in completed collar and lapel.

5) Pin facing to garment; work from collar notch to roll line, centering the ease in facing ½" (1.3 cm) on each side of lower end of lapel roll line. Continue to lower edge of garment; pull facing slightly taut around curve at lower edge so curve will cup against body. Baste if desired.

6) Stitch around collar from collar notch to collar notch; begin and end one stitch from neckline stitching. Shorten stitch length around collar point; stitch two stitches across point. Leave 10" (25 cm) thread tails; do not backstitch. Tie off thread tails at each end of stitching.

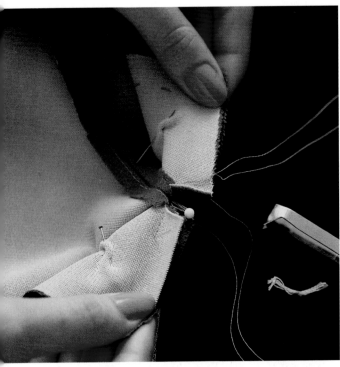

3) Match collar notches carefully; pin through layers at last stitch of neckline seam. Use tweezers to remove tailor's tacks.

4) Thread needle with thread tails at end of neckline seam; bring through to collar notch. Tie all four thread tails together in a secure knot. Remove pin, and trim tails.

7) Stitch from collar notch to lower edge of garment. Begin with 10" (25 cm) thread tail; start one stitch from neckline stitching. Stitch upper seamline of lapel in a slight bow to prevent the illusion of a dip at edge of lapel. Shorten stitch length, and stitch two stitches across point.

8) Stitch remaining side. Compare size and shape of collar and lapel points and the length of fronts to make sure they match. Check stitching accuracy; adjust if necessary. Tie off thread tails. Remove basting.

How to Trim and Press the Collar and Lapels

1) Press seams flat to set stitches. Position seams on point presser or contoured pressing board; press seams open. For rounded collar and lapels, position curves on curve of contoured pressing board or tailor's ham.

2) Clip seam allowance at lower end of roll line. Below clip, grade jacket seam allowance to ¼" (6 mm) and facing to ⅛" (3 mm). Above clip, grade jacket seam allowance to ⅛" (3 mm) and facing to ¼" (6 mm). Trim points, and notch curved seam allowances.

3) Grade upper collar seam allowance to ¼" (6 mm) and undercollar seam allowance to ⅛" (3 mm). Trim points, and notch curved seam allowances. Press all seams open again in collar, lapels, and front edges.

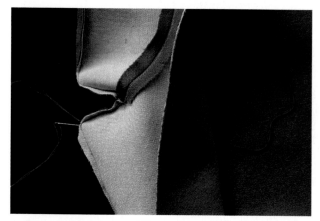

4) Turn right side out. Thread a needle, and draw thread through a stitch in collar or lapel point. Tug thread tails gently to turn point. Or use point turner to push out points; use rounded end of turner to smooth out curves.

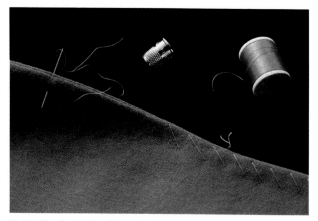

5) Roll edge of collar to underside and edge of lapel toward garment from collar notch to lower end of roll line. Roll edge toward front facing from roll line to lower edge of garment. Hand-baste with silk thread.

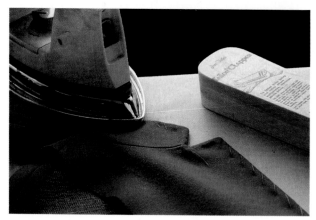

6) Press from center back of collar to lower edge of garment. Working in small sections, steam press basted edges and use clapper. Repeat until edge is smooth, flat, and thin. Allow to dry.

How to Tack the Neckline Seam

1) Smooth collar and lapels in place. Anchor upper collar to undercollar and facing to garment at roll lines, using tailor basting.

2) Attach facing seam to neckline seam with loose running stitch. For garments without a back neck facing, attach seamline of upper collar to neckline seam of garment.

Tailoring a Shawl Collar

Shawl collars require shaping with interfacing and tape, but are easier to tailor than notched collars. The methods used to cut and apply the interfacing and back stay are similar to those for notched collar styles. Hair canvas or fusible interfacing may be used to tailor a shawl collar.

On shawl collar patterns, both the upper and undercollar have a center back seam. In some patterns, the undercollar and the garment front are cut as one piece. In others, the undercollar is separate and must be applied to the front and back neckline.

Select from custom, machine, or fusible methods of tailoring. Interface and shape the undercollar and jacket front according to the method selected. Whichever method of tailoring is used, the shawl collar is constructed in the same way once the interfacing is applied.

How to Shape and Stitch a Shawl Collar

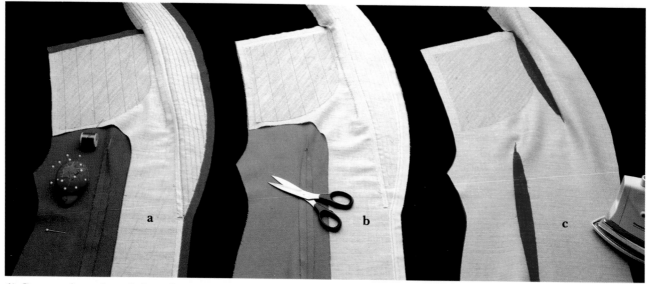

1) Cut, mark, and apply interfacing to undercollar and jacket front as for custom **(a)**, machine **(b)**, or fusible **(c)** method. Stitch the undercollar center back seam. Tape the roll line if desired, stopping at shoulder seam; use custom method, steps 7 and 8, page 70, or machine method, step 4, page 72. For custom method, tape front edge from top buttonhole to lower edge of garment.

2) Staystitch upper collar neck edge on seamline, using smaller reinforcing stitches at inside corners. Clip to stitching at corners. Staystitch back neck facing ½" (1.3 cm) from raw edge; clip.

3) Pin and stitch facing to upper collar. Stitch to corner, spread clips, and pivot. Continue stitching.

4) Cut square from upper collar seam allowance at each corner. Trim seam allowances to ⅜" (1 cm). Press seam open over contoured pressing board or tailor's ham.

5) Stitch upper collar/facing unit to undercollar/ garment unit. Stitch from center back of collar to lower edge of garment. Repeat on other half. Trim and press as for notched collar (page 82).

Tailoring Pockets

Pockets are highly visible fashion details in tailored jackets and coats. They can be functional or purely decorative. They can be as simple as the curved or rectangular patch pocket most often found in blazers, casual coats, and garments with men's styling. Or they can be as complex as a double welt, flap, or single welt pocket. All require attention to detail and careful, accurate stitching to ensure beautiful results.

Once you have mastered the techniques for each type of pocket, it is relatively simple to substitute one type for another. A fabric that ravels may not be ideal for a pattern with double welt pockets, so you may substitute lined patch pockets. If patch pockets add too much bulk at the hipline of a full figure or if the fabric is bulky, straight or slanted double welt pockets are smoother, less bulky alternatives.

Pocket pairs should be identical in size, shape, and position. Whether decorative or functional, they should be placed at a comfortable and flattering position. Check pocket placement on your test garment or when pin-fitting the pattern. Pockets are easiest to sew when the garment fronts are still separate from other parts of the garment.

Machine stitching that is invisible from the outside of the garment can be used for an unlined curved patch pocket with self-facing. This method works best on medium and large pockets and may require practice.

Two Ways to Position a Patch Pocket on a Garment

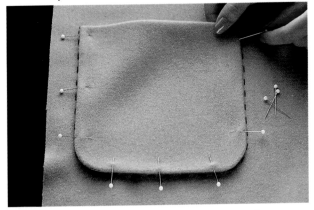

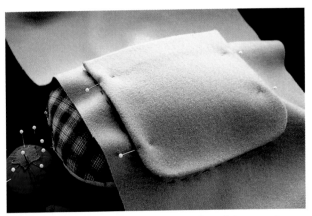

Place completed pocket on garment at pocket placement lines. Place upper corners slightly inside placement line to allow ease for curve of body.

Place garment on tailor's ham, and position pocket. Curve of the ham allows for curve of body.

How to Sew an Unlined Curved Patch Pocket

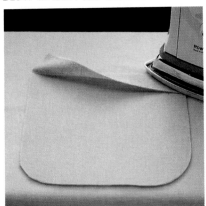

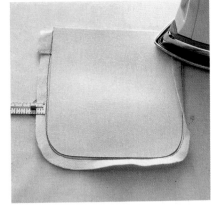

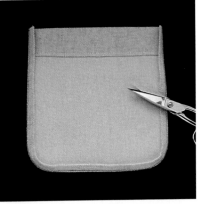

1) Fuse fusible knit interfacing to wrong side of pocket. Overlock or zigzag edge of self-facing. Fold pocket facing to inside, and press.

2) Machine-stitch ½" (1.3 cm) from raw edges, using contrasting thread. Press seam allowance over cardboard template cut to finished pocket size.

3) Trim seam allowance to ¼" (6 mm). If desired, finish raw edges with overlocking or zigzagging to prevent raveling.

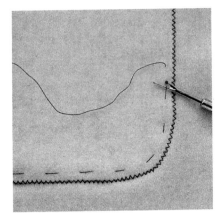

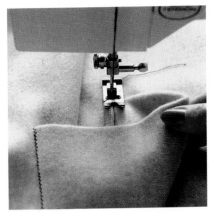

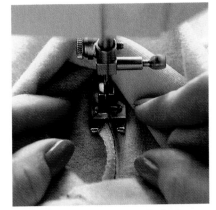

4) Position pocket on garment, as above; hand-baste. Loosen upper tension slightly; barely catch pocket edge with long narrow zigzag stitch. Remove hand basting.

5) Set machine for straight stitching and balanced tension. Working inside pocket, open seam allowance and stitch on the pressed line.

6) Open pocket as you stitch; keep garment smooth under presser foot. Zigzag stitches secure pocket and open up as you stitch. Remove zigzag stitches. Backstitch to reinforce corners.

How to Sew a Lined Patch Pocket

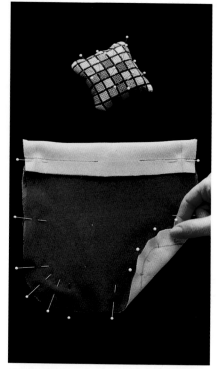

1) Apply interfacing to wrong side of pocket. Mark seamline around a cardboard template cut to the finished pocket size.

2) Stitch lining to self-facing, right sides together; leave opening in center. Trim and press seam toward lining. Trim ⅛" (3 mm) from edge of lining and self-facing; taper to foldline.

3) Pin lining to pocket, right sides together and outer edges matching. Stitch on marked seamline.

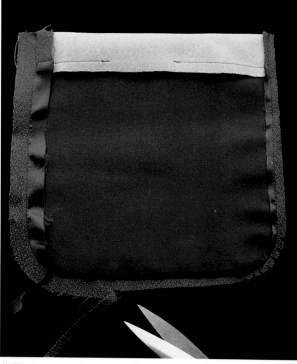

4) Press seam flat; press lining seam allowance toward lining. Trim, clip, and notch seams.

5) Turn pocket right side out; press from lining side, rolling seam toward lining. Close opening with fusible web or slipstitching.

How to Attach a Lined Patch Pocket by Machine

1) Cut ⅛" (3 mm) strip of fusible web, and position just inside edge on underside of completed pocket. Hold steam iron 1" (2.5 cm) away, and steam lightly.

2) Position pocket on garment at placement lines. Cover with press cloth, and fuse with steam for a few seconds.

3) Edgestitch or topstitch ¼" (6 mm) from finished edge. To reinforce corners, zigzag with short stitches, or backstitch.

How to Attach a Lined Patch Pocket by Hand

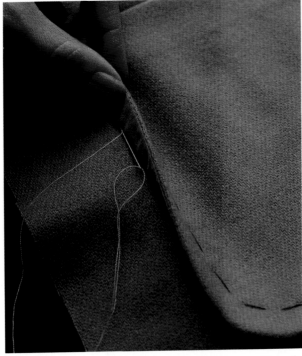 

1) Position completed pocket on garment, and hand-baste ½" (1.3 cm) from finished edge. Roll pocket back to basting line; slipstitch lining to garment.

2) Slipstitch again close to finished edge. To prevent flattened edge, do not pull stitches too tight. Reinforce corners with hand bar tacks (page 44) or invisible stitching. Remove basting.

Welt Pockets

A double welt pocket is a couture detail that requires precise marking, cutting, and stitching. Flap pockets and single welt pockets are variations of the double welt pocket. A single welt pocket is often positioned as a breast pocket but can also be placed in the lower pocket area, either straight or at an angle.

Eliminate the welt and pocket lining pattern pieces if included in your pattern. Flap and single welt pockets require the same pocket lining and underlay pieces and the same pocket placement markings as double welt pockets.

The directions that follow are for 5" (12.5 cm) pockets. It is easy to change the size of a welt pocket. For a double welt pocket, simply cut the welts the desired finished length of the pocket plus 1½" (3.8 cm); the welts are always cut 1⅛" (2.7 cm) in depth. For a single welt pocket, cut the welt the desired finished length of the pocket plus ½" (1.3 cm); cut the depth two times the finished depth plus 1" (2.5 cm).

If using fusible interfacing, apply the interfacing before attaching the pocket. If using hair canvas, attach the pocket first. The area behind the pocket may be backed with lightweight fusible interfacing for stability. A muslin strip extending from a lower welt pocket to the armhole gives support to the pocket and prevents gaping and pulling at the pocket opening.

Welt and flap pockets may cross a dart or seam but should never end at one. Always do a test pocket to determine suitability for the fabric you are using and to master the technique.

How to Stay and Mark a Welt Pocket

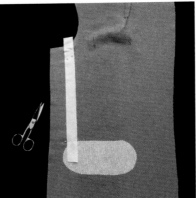

1) Reinforce area behind the pocket with a pinked oval of lightweight fusible interfacing. Before fusing, remove all but one strand of floss from pocket tailor's tacks.

2) Cut a 1" × 15" (2.5 × 38 cm) strip of muslin on straight grain for each pocket (except breast pockets). Center over end of placement line from center line to armhole. Baste; trim excess at armhole.

3) Mark pocket position on right side of garment, using sharpened wax chalk and see-through ruler. Mark center and ends of placement lines. Baste in contrasting thread if chalk will not mark.

How to Cut Pocket Welts and Lining

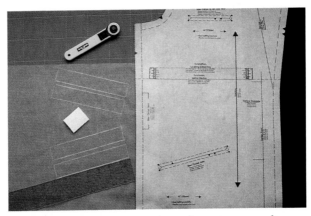

1a) Straight pocket. For each pocket, cut two welts from garment fabric, 1⅛" × 6½" (2.7 × 16.3 cm), on crosswise grain.

1b) Angled pocket. For each pocket, cut two welts, 1⅛" × 6½" (2.7 × 16.3 cm); cut at the same angle on crosswise grain as the pocket placement line.

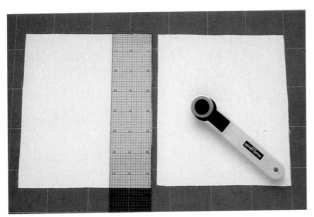

2) Cut two lining pieces for each pocket from lining or pocketing fabric (page 27). Lining pieces should measure 6½" × 7½" (16.3 × 19.3 cm).

3) Cut a 2" × 6½" (5 × 16.3 cm) strip of garment fabric for pocket underlay for each pocket. Position underlay on right side of one lining piece, with upper edges even. Baste ¼" (6 mm) from upper edge, and zigzag lower edge of underlay to lining.

How to Sew a Double Welt

1) Steam press pocket welts while stretching. Repeat several times to remove all stretch and eliminate puckering in completed welt.

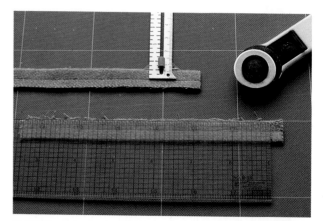

2) Fold and press welts lengthwise, with wrong sides together and raw edges matching. Machine-baste exactly ¼" (6 mm) from fold for stitching guideline. Trim raw edges to scant ¼" (6 mm) from stitching.

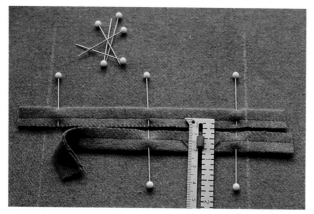

3) Position welts on garment fronts, with raw edges meeting on centerline of pocket marking; stitching lines must be placed ½" (1.3 cm) apart. Pin welts in place. Mark ends of placement lines on welts.

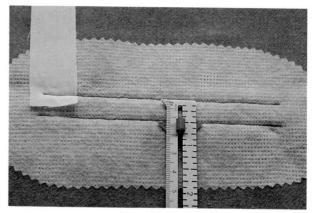

4) Stitch from right side precisely on stitching guidelines, using 20 stitches per inch (2.5 cm). Begin and end stitching exactly at ends of placement lines; backstitch to secure. Check stitching from wrong side for accuracy; adjust if necessary. Press.

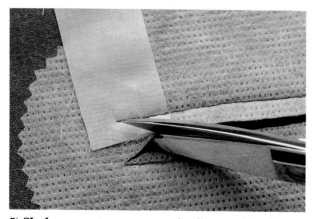

5) Slash garment on center pocket line, working from wrong side; stop ½" (1.3 cm) from each end. Do not cut welts. Cut remainder of opening at an angle, clipping to, but not through, the last stitch. If fabric is loosely woven, treat clipped edges at corners with liquid fray preventer.

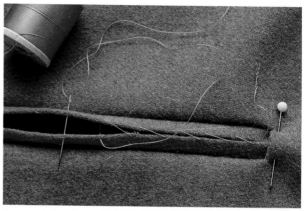

6) Turn welts to inside and adjust in opening so they are straight and even. If corners pucker and welts do not lie flat, carefully turn welts back to outside and clip closer to stitches at each corner. Tailor-baste welts together with silk thread; press. Leave basting in place until garment is completed.

How to Attach a Double Welt Pocket Lining

1) Lay lining piece without underlay over welts, with raw edge of lining even with raw edge of lower welt.

2) Stitch, with lining side down, along previous stitching line. Fold lining down, and press.

3) Stitch lining/underlay to edge of upper welt, with underlay against welt; follow previous stitching line. Lower edges of lining are not even.

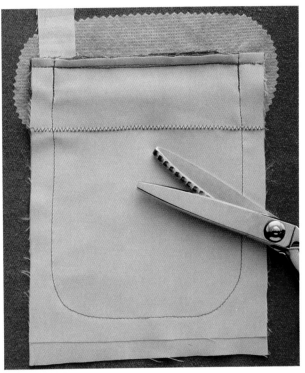

4) Fold garment back to expose welts, and machine-baste through base of triangles. Check ends on right side of garment to make sure stitching is straight and corners are secure.

5) Stitch lining pieces together with ¾" (2 cm) seam allowance. Stitch over triangles several times to reinforce; round off lower corners. Press. Pink outer edges of lining.

How to Sew a Single Welt Pocket

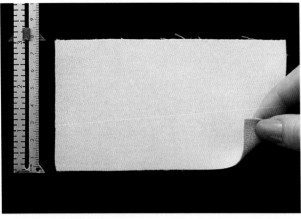

1) Cut one welt from garment fabric 5½" × 3" (14 × 7.5 cm) for each pocket. Interface welt with the lightweight fusible interfacing.

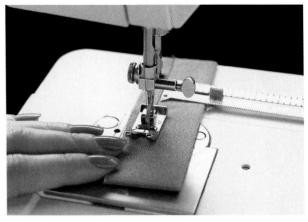

2) Fold welt lengthwise, with right sides together and raw edges even. Stitch ¼" (6 mm) seams at ends of welt; trim. Turn welt right side out; press. Baste stitching guideline 1" (2.5 cm) from fold.

3) Position welt on garment, right sides together, with raw edges at pocket center line and with fold toward lower edge of garment. Follow steps 2 and 3, page 91, to cut and sew pocket and underlay pieces. Pin lining/underlay piece on garment, with underlay against garment and raw edges at center line.

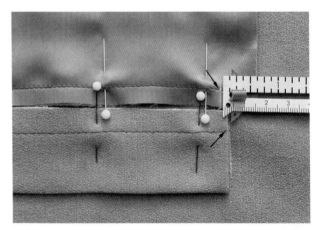

4) Mark ends of stitching lines on lining/underlay ⅛" (3 mm) in from ends of welt. Stitch lining/underlay and welt in place on stitching guidelines; begin and end stitching exactly at ends of welt and at ends of marked guideline on lining/underlay (arrows).

5) Slash and clip garment as in step 5, page 92. Turn lining/underlay to inside through slash, and press welt up over opening.

6) Complete pocket lining, as in steps 1, 2, 4, and 5, page 93. Fellstitch or edgestitch ends of welt to garment.

How to Sew a Welt Pocket with a Flap

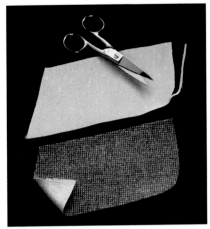

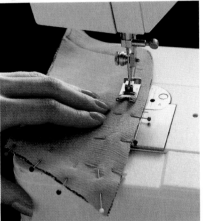

1) Use pattern to cut flap from garment fabric and lining. Trim ⅛" (3 mm) from outer edges of lining so seam will roll under. If desired, fuse lightweight interfacing to wrong side of flap.

2) Pin flap and lining, right sides together, forcing edges to match. Using short stitches, stitch lining to flap, leaving upper edge open.

3) Press seam flat; press lining seam allowance toward lining. Trim and grade seam allowances; clip, turn, and press. The seam rolls under slightly. Baste raw edges together.

4) Cut and sew double welt pocket (pages 91 and 92); do not baste welts together. Slip flap into welt opening.

5) Pin flap, aligning flap seamline with welt opening (arrow); baste. Complete pocket (page 93).

How to Add a Pocket to Jacket Lining

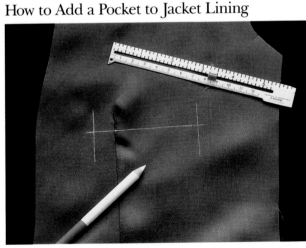

1) Add one or more welt pockets to right lining front. Determine desired position and size; mark placement.

2) Sew single or double welt pocket (pages 90 to 94). Use for lipstick, theater tickets, or passport.

Tailoring Sleeves

A smooth sleeve with a softly rounded cap is a true mark of an expertly tailored jacket or coat. Special sewing techniques make it possible to ease a sleeve into an armhole without making visible tucks. Wool fabrics ease into the armhole seam more readily than others because excess fullness can be minimized with steam pressing. Before setting in sleeves, stitch all seams in the body of the garment.

Use one of the following two methods to set in sleeves. The first is an adaptation of the standard ease-stitched method. For this method, stitch three rows of easestitching instead of the usual two, spacing rows ¼", ½", and ¾" (6 mm, 1.3 cm, and 2 cm) from the raw edge of the sleeve cap from notch to notch. If the fabric needle-marks, place the third row ⅝" (1.5 cm) from the edge. Pull up the bobbin threads and adjust the ease in the sleeve cap. A small amount of ease should be at the top, with most of the ease between the top of the sleeve and the small dots between the top and notches.

The second method uses a true bias strip of lambswool, hair canvas, or self-fabric to control fullness. This method is suitable for any tailoring fabric. It is highly recommended for fabrics that are difficult to ease or when it is difficult to shrink out fullness with steam. Use self-fabric strips for unlined garments.

Add a sleeve head after the sleeve is set in to support the sleeve cap and to prevent the edge of the seam allowance from showing on the right side. A sleeve head is usually not necessary when the sleeve is set in with the bias strip method. Do not add a sleeve head in dropped-shoulder sleeves.

How to Sew a Set-in Sleeve with Easestitching

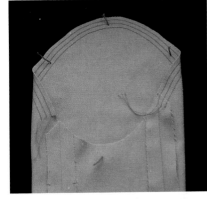

1) Easestitch around sleeve cap as described, opposite. Loosen tension; stitch on right side of sleeve 10 stitches per inch (2.5 cm).

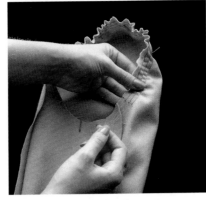

2) Draw up bobbin thread, estimating amount of ease. Adjust ease in sleeve cap as described, opposite. To test sleeve shape, cup fingers under sleeve cap.

3) Pin sleeve into armhole, matching markings and raw edges. Ease underarm section slightly. When pinning around cap, hold garment over fingers so sleeve turns back; adjust ease.

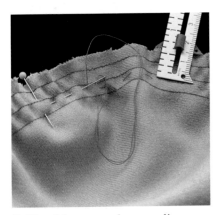

4) Hand-baste on the seamline, using small stitches. Try on with shoulder pads in place; adjust set and hang of sleeve (page 52).

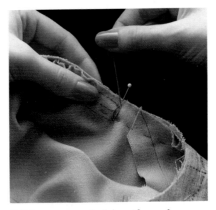

5) Wrap easestitching threads around pin. If sleeve cap puckers, remove sleeve. Shrink out ease over tailor's ham, holding iron just above fabric; steam. Allow to dry. Repeat steps 3 and 4.

6) Stitch sleeve, garment side up. Start at notch; stitch underarm, around cap, and back to beginning notch. Stitch a second row ⅛" (3 mm) from first in underarm seam allowance between notches.

7) Check sleeve on outside for smooth, pucker-free stitching; adjust if necessary. Remove hand basting on inside and any machine basting that shows on the outside. Trim the underarm to ¼" (6 mm) between notches. Trim the remainder to ½" (1.3 cm).

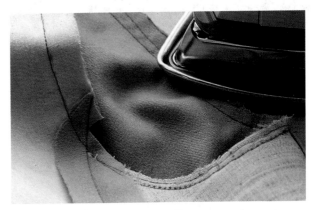

8) Press the sleeve cap seam allowance only, up to ⅛" (3 mm) beyond seamline into cap to prevent a flattened sleeve cap. Do not press underarm curve.

How to Sew a Set-in Sleeve with Bias Strip

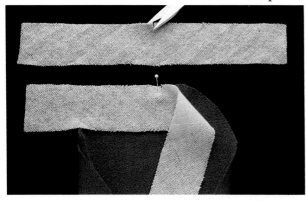

1) Cut two 2" × 12" (5 × 30.5 cm) true bias strips of lambswool. Snip-mark center of each strip. Use one pin to secure bias strip to wrong side at top of sleeve cap, with raw edges matching.

2) Insert needle at pin, and stitch bias strip to cap ½" (1.3 cm) from raw edge. Fully stretch bias strip while stitching from top of cap to small dot. At same time, ease fabric, gently pushing it under presser foot. At dot, stop easing fabric but continue stretching bias strip. End stitching at notch.

3) Repeat on other half of sleeve. If machine does not have marked stitching gauge to left of needle, mark ½" (1.3 cm) gauge with tape on bed of machine. Trim away any excess bias strip below notches.

4) Pin sleeve into garment. If sleeve is larger than armhole, distribute ease and pin liberally. If sleeve is smaller than armhole, snip every sixth stitch and release fullness. Stitch and press sleeves, steps 6 to 8, page 97.

How to Add a Sleeve Head

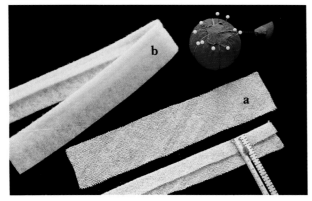

1) Cut a 2" × 9" (5 × 23 cm) bias strip of lambswool or heavy flannel for each sleeve **(a)**. Fold ⅝" (1.5 cm) from one long edge of head. Or use nonwoven purchased sleeve head **(b)**.

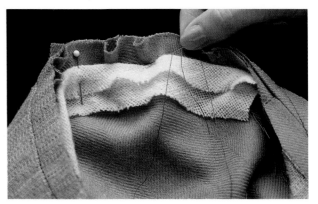

2) Center sleeve head in the sleeve cap, and slipstitch the folded edge to the sleeve seam.

How to Attach Shoulder Pads (for set-in sleeves)

1) Use standard shoulder pads (page 26). Pin into garment, with pad extending ½" (1.3 cm) beyond seamline. Try on garment; adjust placement for smooth fit.

2) Attach pad to shoulder seam allowance, using loose stitches. Do not stitch through all layers of pad.

3) Smooth garment over pad. Tack lower edge of pad to armhole seam allowance, using loose stitches.

How to Attach Shoulder Pads (for dropped shoulders)

 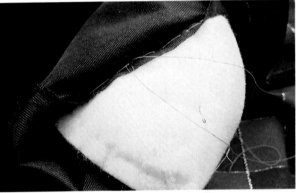

1) Use raglan shoulder pads (page 26). Try on the garment. Position pad so sleeve hangs straight from shoulder. Pin pad in place.

2) Attach pad to shoulder seam allowance, using loose stitches. Do not stitch through all layers of pad.

How to Attach Shoulder Pads (for raglan sleeves)

 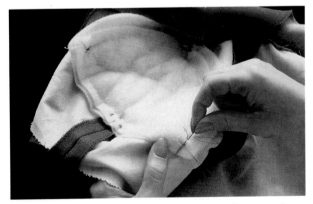

1) Use raglan shoulder pads (page 26). Try on the garment. Position pad so sleeve hangs straight from shoulder. Pin pad in place.

2) Tack pad to raglan sleeve stay (page 57), or tack to shoulder seam or dart.

Tailored Hems

Hems in the sleeves and lower edges of tailored garments are interfaced with strips of interfacing to add body and to support the weight of the hem. Interfacing also adds strength and prevents stretching in hem edges, which are subject to wear. When hems are interfaced, hemming stitches and the edge of the hem do not show through to the right side. If using woven or weft-insertion fusible interfacing or hair canvas interfacing, cut strips on the true bias. If using fusible knit or nonwoven fusible interfacing, cut strips so the crosswise stretch goes around the body.

For the custom method, interfacing in tailored hems extends ½" (1.3 cm) beyond the hemline into the *hem allowance* to cushion the edge for a softer fold. Cut hair canvas strips the width of the hem allowance plus 1½" (3.8 cm). Piece the strips to fit the circumference of the hem plus 1" (2.5 cm) for overlap at front interfacing.

For the fusible method, interfacing extends ½" (1.3 cm) beyond the hemline into the *garment*. Cut fusible

interfacing strips ½" (1.3 cm) wider than the hem allowance and the length of each section of the hem between seam allowances. Allow ¼" (6 mm) extra on each strip that overlaps the front interfacing. Pink one long edge of the interfacing strips.

Try on the garment to determine the finished length of the sleeves and of the garment. The finished sleeve should cover the wristbone by ½" to 1" (1.3 to 2.5 cm). Pin hems, and trim to an even width. In buttoned styles the underlap side should be slightly shorter than the overlap.

For a thin and crisp finished edge, miter the corner in the overlaps of sleeve and back vents to reduce the layers. The sleeves can be mitered and hemmed before they are set into the armhole if the correct length was determined in a test garment. If not, set the sleeves in first, check the length, and then hem using the mitering technique (page 103).

How to Hem a Jacket or Coat (custom method)

1) Press a light crease at hem fold. Turn up ⅛" (3 mm) extra in front facing, tapering to the front seam so facing edge will not show from the outside when hemmed. Trim seams.

2) Easestitch ¼" (6 mm) from hem edge. To remove slight fullness, draw up stitching and adjust ease so hem edge lies loosely against garment. Tuck paper strips under hem allowance; steam hem edge lightly to shrink out fullness.

3) Place a pin in the hem allowance 1" (2.5 cm) inside the raw edge of the front facing.

4) Trim facing hem allowance ½" (1.3 cm) below hemline. Trim garment ¾" (2 cm) below hemline from facing seamline to pin in hem allowance. Clip and press seam toward facing in hem allowance.

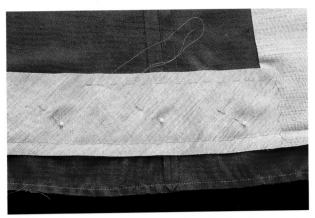

5) Cut hair canvas strips, opposite. Pin in place, with ½" (1.3 cm) extending past hemline. Catchstitch to front interfacing. Use permanent uneven basting stitches in hemline and temporary basting ½" (1.3 cm) from upper raw edge of strips to secure strip to garment.

6) Turn back upper edge of strip ¼" (6 mm), and stitch to garment with invisible tailor's hemstitch. Use matching thread, and do not pull stitches tight. Remove basting at upper edge of strip.

7) Turn hem up, and press. Use clapper to flatten facing hem. Baste ½" (1.3 cm) from hemline. Attach raw edge of hem to interfacing with permanent uneven basting.

8) Turn facing to inside of garment. Attach raw edge of facing to garment hem allowance with fellstitches. For fabrics that ravel, apply liquid fray preventer.

How to Hem a Jacket or Coat (fusible method)

1) Prepare hem as in step 1, opposite. Fuse interfacing strips (opposite) to hem allowance, with pinked edge extending into garment ½" (1.3 cm) past hemline. Fuse ends under seam allowances.

2) Complete hemming preparations as in steps 2 to 4, opposite. Turn hem up, and press; pink raw edges. Baste hem to garment ½" (1.3 cm) below edge. Use tailor's hemstitch, catching only a thread of garment in stitches. Complete hem as in step 8, above.

How to Miter and Hem a Back Vent

1) Reinforce vent corner on right back, using short stitches just inside seamline. Stitch center back seam; clip right back seam allowance to dot. Press overlap toward left back, creasing foldline. Press under seam allowance on underlap. Press a light crease at hemline, with underlap ⅛" (3 mm) shorter than overlap.

2) Interface vent. If using bias hair canvas **(a)**, cut 1" (2.5 cm) wider and longer than overlap; extend ½" (1.3 cm) past upper edge of vent and foldlines of vent and hem. Secure with permanent uneven basting. Interface hem, step 5, page 101. If using fusible interfacing **(b)**, cut ½" (1.3 cm) wider and 1" (2.5 cm) longer than overlap. Fuse to vent self-facing; extend ½" (1.3 cm) past upper edge of vent and foldlines of vent and hem. Interface hem, step 1, page 101.

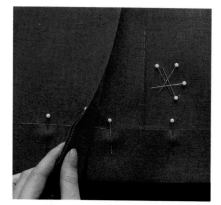

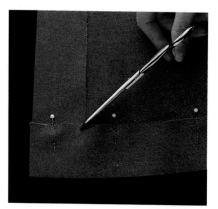

3) Arrange the vent in wearing position. Turn up, pin, and press hem as creased in step 1, above.

4) Clip overlap and hem allowance where edges meet.

5) Open out corner. Mark stitching line from clips, marking through corner where pressed lines meet.

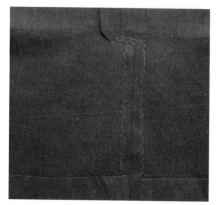

6) Fold on diagonal, with right sides together and clips matching. Stitch on marked line; trim. Press seam open. Turn right side out.

7) Fold underlap hem to outside. Stitch on seamline from fold to hem edge; grade. Press seam open. Turn right side out, and press.

8) Baste vent in wearing position. Machine-stitch across upper edge of vent through all layers; grade seam. Catchstitch vent edges. Stitch hem.

How to Miter and Hem a Sleeve Vent

 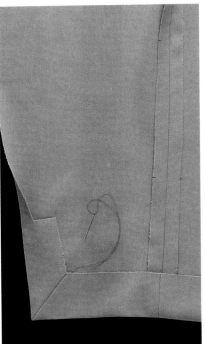 

1) Stitch upper sleeve to under sleeve; leave seam with vent open. Press foldlines of vent and hem. Cut and apply hair canvas **(a)** or fusible **(b)** interfacing (page 101); do not extend hair canvas into vent underlap.

2) Fold vent overlap to inside; turn up hem allowance. Complete as for back vent, steps 4 to 6, opposite. Hand-stitch hem.

3) Stitch seam with vent; clip the underlap seam allowance to dot. Press seam open. Catchstitch upper edge and sides of vent. Sew buttons on the right side of overlap at the pattern markings.

How to Prepare a Garment for Lining

1) Turn facing back and anchor to tape at roll line, using small invisible stitches. If bound buttonholes are used, finish backs, step 15, page 119.

2) Catchstitch outer edges of facing to interfacing unless lining is to be attached by machine. Press garment, as needed, before applying lining.

Finishing Techniques

Linings

Tailored jackets and coats are usually lined. A lining covers the interfacing layers and other details of inner construction. It eliminates the need for time-consuming seam finishes and reduces friction between the jacket or coat and the garments worn beneath it. A lining takes most of the wearing strain, lengthening the life and durability of the finished jacket or coat. Piping can be added between the lining and the facing as a special finishing detail.

The custom method for setting in a lining combines machine-stitching the lining pieces together, then hand-sewing the lining into the garment.

Setting in the lining by machine is a faster method. In this method, lining sleeves are machine-stitched to the garment at the hem. Even when the lining is set in by machine, the sleeves should be set into the armhole by hand to anchor the body lining and sleeve lining to the jacket for better fit and wearability. For either the custom or machine method, cut the lining pieces as directed on pages 58 and 59.

How to Attach a Lining (custom method)

1) Staystitch front, neck, and shoulder edges of lining. Stitch and press all lengthwise seams in body of lining and sleeve linings. Stitch back darts if included; press. Turn under and press seam allowances on lining front; clip so they lie flat.

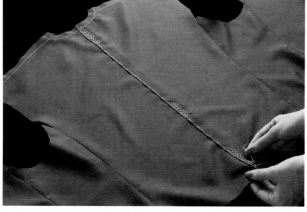

2) Baste on center back line, and press pleat toward left back. Featherstitch or catchstitch pleat through all layers at neckline, waist, and lower edge for 2" to 3" (5 to 7.5 cm). Remove basting.

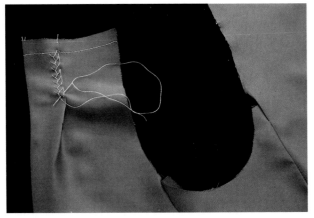

3) Baste any tucks or darts at shoulders and waistline; press. At shoulders, featherstitch or catchstitch for 2" (5 cm) from raw edge. At waist, featherstitch for 2" (5 cm) at center of tuck or dart. Remove basting.

4) Stitch side seam allowances of lining and garment together with long, loose running stitches. End stitching 4" (10 cm) from lower edge of garment. Omit this step in coats.

5) Clip back neck seam allowance; turn under and pin to back neckline. Smooth and pin lining around armholes; start at underarm, and work to shoulder seam. Turn under back shoulder seam allowance, and lap over front; pin. Baste back neckline and shoulder seams.

6) Lap front edges of lining over facing at seamline. Pin through facing only, beginning and ending 4" (10 cm) above hemline. To ease lining at bustline curve, place work over tailor's ham while pinning lining to facing. Hand-baste.

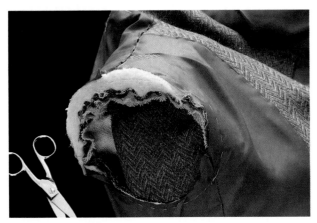

7) Hand-stitch lining around armhole a scant ⅝" (1.5 cm) from the edge. Loosely hand-stitch lining to shoulder pad and sleeve seam allowance. Between notches, trim underarm of lining to match underarm of garment.

8) Try on jacket, and check for smooth fit. If lining is too tight, it will pull on jacket, creating wrinkles and lines. Release basting as necessary to adjust lining, and baste again. Slipstitch all lining edges in place with short, invisible stitches. Remove basting.

How to Set In a Sleeve Lining

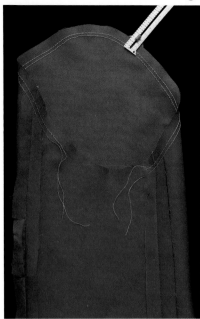

1) Easestitch lining sleeve cap between notches ⅜" (1 cm) and a scant ⅝" (1.5 cm) from raw edge.

2) Slip lining into garment sleeve, wrong sides together. Turn under ¼" (6 mm) at underarm between notches, and pin to seamline. Turn under seam allowance at top of cap, and pin to armhole seamline.

3) Draw up threads to ease lining to fit sleeve; turn under lining edges. Pin. Fellstitch sleeve lining to armhole lining, using two strands of waxed thread. Do not catch garment in the stitching.

How to Hem a Jacket or Sleeve Lining

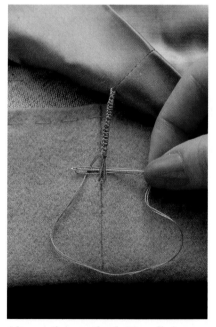

1) Pin lining to garment 3" (7.5 cm) above hem. Trim lining so it is ⅝" (1.5 cm) longer than finished jacket. Fold lining edge under ⅝" (1.5 cm). Pin folded edge of lining so it just covers hem edge. Slipstitch; remove pins.

2) Allow lining hem to drop down, forming jump pleat for wearing ease at lower edge of jacket or sleeve. Slipstitch front edge of lining to facing at lower edge. Press hem.

Alternative method. Hem lining 1" (2.5 cm) shorter than finished garment. Slipstitch front edge of lining to facing at lower edge. At seams, use swing tacks, taking three or four stitches 2" (5 cm) long and covering with blanket stitches as for bar tack, page 44.

How to Attach a Lining (machine method)

1) Stitch and press all seams in lining body. Easestitch lining sleeve cap between notches ⅜" (1 cm) and a scant ⅝" (1.5 cm) from raw edge. Follow steps 2 and 3, pages 106 and 107, for back pleat and tucks or darts.

2) Clip lining at neckline; machine-stitch lining to front and back neck facing. Begin and end stitching 4" (10 cm) above hemline. Press seam toward lining.

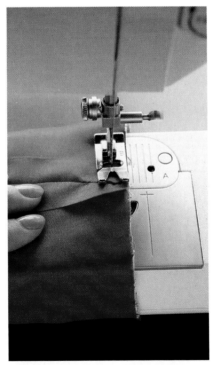

3) Attach lining side seams to garment seams from inside, using loose running stitches; end stitching 4" (10 cm) from lower edge. Stitch lining at armholes, step 7, page 107. Hem garment, opposite.

4) Join lower edge of lining sleeve to lower edge of garment sleeve, right sides together, with ¼" (6 mm) seam. Use free arm of machine, if it is available.

5) Turn garment right side out, and pull sleeve lining into sleeve. Set in sleeve lining, steps 2 and 3, opposite. Stitch in the ditch at lower edge of sleeve seams; end stitching at lining.

How to Attach a Lining with a Back Vent

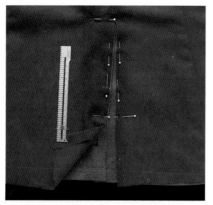

1) Construct lining, steps 1 to 3, pages 106 to 107. On cutting lines, cut away left back vent in lining. Reinforce corner in left vent, using short stitches; clip to stitching.

2) Press under seam allowance in left vent; press under ¾" (2 cm) on right vent. Attach lining, steps 4 to 7, page 107. Pin lining to vents, ending 4" (10 cm) from lower edge.

3) Hem lining, forming jump pleat, and slipstitch vent lining edges to vent as for front lining, steps 1 and 2, page 108.

How to Make and Insert Piping in Lining

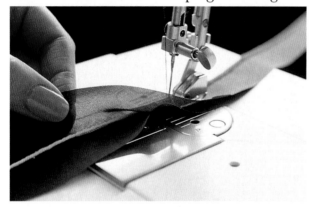

1) Cut 1¾" (4.5 cm) bias strips of lining the length of front facings and back neck facing, if included, plus 3" (7.5 cm). Fold strip around ³⁄₃₂" cording or yarn. While stretching cording, stitch close to cording, using zipper foot.

2) Pin piping to right side of facing, with end of piping at finished edge of jacket. Machine-baste on stitching line, starting and ending as close to the top edge of the hem as possible.

3) Machine-stitch facing to lining, with right sides together and facing side up; crowd cording. Hem lining. Turn end of piping under to match length of lining; slipstitch lining and piping in place. Press seam allowances toward lining.

4) Garment without back neck facing. Pin lining to armholes and back neckline. Turn under back shoulder seam allowance, and lap over front; baste. Slipstitch neckline and shoulder seams.

Interlining a Jacket or Coat

In colder climates, it may be desirable to purchase an insulated lining fabric (page 25) or to include an extra layer of fabric in the lining for an outerwear jacket or coat. Because the extra layer lies between the lining and the garment, it is called an interlining.

For the interlining, choose a lightweight fabric with insulating qualities, such as outing flannel, pajama flannel, or lambswool. The napped surface of flannel and the open weave of lambswool trap air. The lining pattern pieces can be used for cutting the interlining.

Since jacket and coat patterns generally do not allow for interlinings, it is important to adjust the fit of the garment to allow extra room and fitting ease. This is an important consideration in fitted styles, because the extra layer of fabric will use up some of the wearing and design ease. For this reason, do not interline the sleeves unless the interlining is thin or the sleeve has a full cut. When interlining a coat, the interlining is trimmed from seam and hem allowances to eliminate bulk.

How to Interline a Jacket or Coat

1) Cut interlining, using lining front and back pattern pieces. Fold under center back ease pleat on pattern piece; transfer markings.

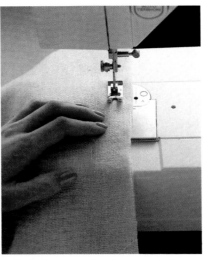

2) Stitch center back seam and darts in interlining. Or eliminate center back seam for straight styles by placing seamline on fold when cutting fabric.

3) Complete center back pleat in lining, as in step 2, page 106. Stitch darts in lining.

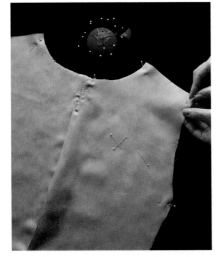

4) Smooth and pin interlining to lining pieces; machine-baste ½" (1.3 cm) from raw edges, with lining side up to prevent slippage.

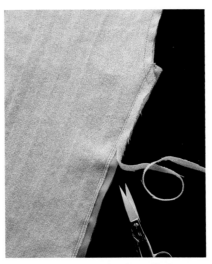

5) Stitch seams; trim interlining close to stitching. Press seams open. Attach lining to garment (pages 106 to 109). Press hemline.

6) Trim interlining to hemline; baste. Machine-stitch lining hem; remove basting. Finish hem as for alternative method on page 108.

Partially Lined Jackets

A partially lined jacket is cooler to wear than a fully lined one. Cut the partial lining as on page 59, using lining fabric for the shaped back piece and extending the front facing to the side seams. Finish exposed seams and facing and hem edges in unlined or partially lined jackets to prevent raveling. Allow 1" (2.5 cm) seam allowances when cutting the jacket to make seams easier to handle when finishing. Choose a finish appropriate to the weight of the fabric.

A Hong Kong seam finish is a quality finish in a tailored garment, but it is more time-consuming than other seam finishes. An edgestitched seam finish can be stitched on any straight-stitch sewing machine. An overlocked seam finish sewn on a serger is the least bulky alternative. If fitting changes are made in a test garment before the garment is cut, finish garment seam allowances before stitching the seams because it is easier to handle single layers of fabric.

Three Ways to Finish Seams

Edgestitched. Stitch ¼" (6 mm) from raw edge for light to mediumweight fabrics. Turn under edge on stitching line. Edgestitch close to fold.

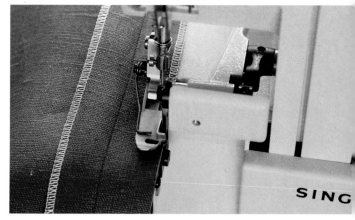

Overlocked. Overlock single seam allowances on serger. Use decorative thread, such as shiny rayon, for special edge finish.

How to Attach a Partial Lining

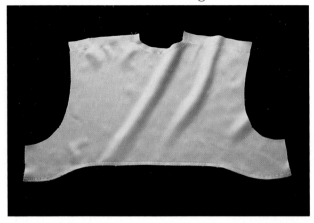

1) Staystitch neck and shoulder edges of back lining; stitch ¼" (6 mm) from lower edge. Press a ¼" (6 mm) hem on lower edge, turning under twice; topstitch.

2) Finish seam on inner edge of front facing, trimming raw edge of facing as needed. (Finished edges of front facing and back lining should meet.) Machine-stitch side seam of front facing and lining back, right sides together; press seam toward back.

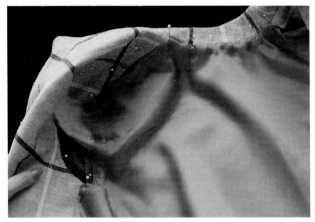

3) Clip neckline so it lies flat; turn under seam allowances on shoulder seams and back neckline. Pin lining at neckline, shoulders, and armholes. Slipstitch neckline and shoulders; baste armholes.

4) Stitch side seam allowances of lining and garment together, using long, loose running stitches. Slipstitch lower edge of facing at hemline. Attach and hem lining sleeves as on page 108.

Hong Kong. 1) Stitch 1" (2.5 cm) bias strip to seam allowance ⅛" (3 mm) from raw edge, stretching tape slightly. Press binding over raw edge as shown.

2) Wrap bias tape around raw edge to the underside; stitch in the ditch of the seam. Trim excess tape ¼" (6 mm) from stitching.

How to Topstitch a Jacket or Coat

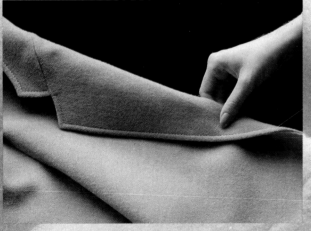

1) Begin topstitching on right side of lapel at lower end of roll line. Pivot at lapel point and again at collar notch.

2) Pivot, and stitch in ditch of seam (arrow). Shorten stitches in ditch to make them less noticeable. Pivot, and continue to topstitch around collar and remaining lapel. End at lower end of other roll line.

Topstitching

Topstitching is a decorative detail that also holds the collar and facing flat. This stitching should be done before buttons are attached. Topstitching placed ¼" (6 mm) from the finished outer edge is standard on blazers and sport coats, but several rows may be used. On thick coating fabrics, stitching farther from the finished edge is also appropriate.

Edgestitching placed close to the outer edges of the garment is especially attractive on hard-surfaced fabrics, such as linen and wool gabardine. If topstitching or edgestitching is used on the outer edges, it is often repeated on pockets or other areas.

Use a heavier thread, such as buttonhole twist, to make stitching more apparent. Try lengthening the stitch for greater stitch definition. To prevent fraying and skipped stitches, be sure to use a special topstitching needle or a size 16 (100) regular machine needle when sewing with heavier thread. When buttonhole twist is not available in the appropriate color, thread one machine needle with two spools of all-purpose thread. Test the stitch length, the thread, and the distance from the edge, using a sample from the same fabric and interfacing layers as those in the garment.

Press the garment, using a clapper on the edges to be topstitched to flatten them as much as possible before topstitching. To keep the stitching straight and even, use the needle plate guide or the edge of the presser foot, or mark stitching lines with transparent tape. When topstitching, stitch slowly; even the tiniest stitch variation will show.

3) Topstitch remainder of front edge with right side of garment up. Begin at lower end of roll line, and stitch to lower edge of jacket. Pivot at end of facing; stitch to edge.

4) Pull threads to facing side. Thread the ends into needle, and bury between garment and facing layers.

Buttons & Buttonholes

Beautiful buttons and expertly sewn buttonholes are the finishing touches on a finely tailored jacket or coat. Use covered snaps on inside areas that will show when the garment is worn open.

Buttons on tailored garments must have a shank that lifts the button away from the thickness of the garment layer to prevent buttonhole strain. Make a thread shank for a sew-through button as it is stitched to the garment. A shank is not necessary if the button is purely decorative such as inner, nonfunctioning buttons on a double-breasted closure.

Bound buttonholes and machine-worked buttonholes are interchangeable on tailored jackets and coats. Bound buttonholes take time to perfect. Make several test samples to check the finished length; and before attempting bound buttonholes on the garment front, master the technique in the fabric you are using.

In custom tailoring, make bound buttonholes in the garment front before attaching hair canvas interfacing. If using the fusible method of tailoring, make bound buttonholes after applying the interfacing. Make machine-worked buttonholes after the garment is completed.

Standards of Bound Buttonholes

Length of buttonhole is at least 1" (2.5 cm); length accommodates button comfortably.

Buttonholes are all uniform in length.

Width of buttonhole is a scant ¼" (6 mm).

Placement is ⅛" (3 mm) beyond the center front line, toward the front edge of the garment.

Spacing between buttonholes is even.

How to Prepare the Garment Front for Bound Buttonholes

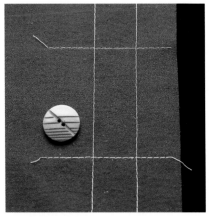

1) Determine buttonhole length. Add the button diameter plus thickness and an extra ⅛" to ¼" (3 to 6 mm) for ease. Make a sample buttonhole to test button fit.

2) Mark center and ends of each buttonhole with basting in contrasting thread, creating a thread ladder on garment front. (For fusible method, apply interfacing before marking.)

3) Pink a small oval patch of lightweight fusible interfacing for custom or machine method. Fuse to wrong side over each buttonhole marking.

How to Make a Bound Buttonhole

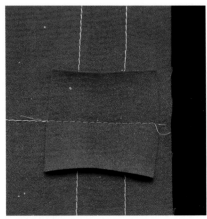

1) Cut a 2½" (6.5 cm) bias square for each buttonhole. Tug, and steam press to remove all stretch.

2) Center and baste the bias square on right side of garment over the buttonhole location.

3) Mark stitching lines on wrong side, ⅛" (3 mm) on each side of center line.

4) Stitch on marked lines, using 20 stitches per inch (2.5 cm). Start and end stitching exactly at buttonhole markings. Leave 4" (10 cm) thread tails.

5) Check that stitching lines are ¼" (6 mm) apart and end exactly at markings. Tie thread tails, but do not clip. Remove center basting, and press square flat.

(Continued on next page)

6) Cut across center of square, being careful not to cut garment.

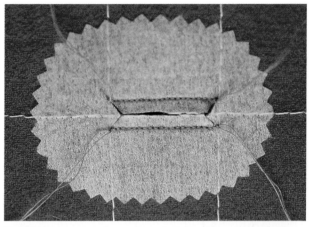

7) Slash garment between stitching lines. Clip to, but not through, corners. Apply liquid fray preventer to cut edges; test on scrap first.

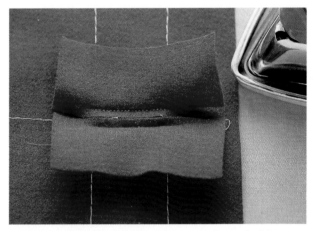

8) Press top half of square down against stitching line; press bottom half up.

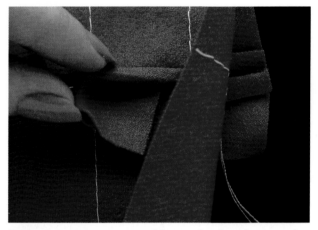

9) Turn square to wrong side; push triangles at ends to wrong side. Adjust lips to equal width, filling opening; press.

10) Cord buttonhole lips with yarn, if desired, by placing yarn close to pressed folds. Cording buttonholes adds strength and stability to lightweight fabrics.

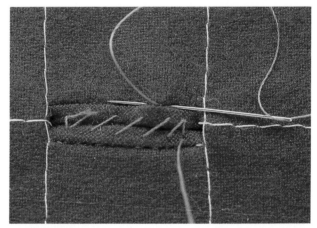

11) Tailor-baste lips together. Stitch in the ditch on both long sides of buttonhole, using a small backstitch. If buttonholes are corded, do not catch yarn in stitching.

12) Turn garment back on itself; stitch through base of triangle at each end of buttonhole, using a short stitch. Check right side. If necessary, stitch several times to secure triangle.

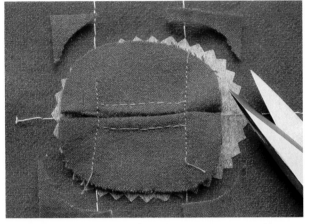

13) Trim the thread tails. Trim square, rounding off the corners. Press completed buttonhole on padded surface.

14) Attach hair canvas for custom or machine method. Pin-mark buttonhole in four corners. Cut rectangle from hair canvas, and pull square through opening. Catchstitch to hair canvas.

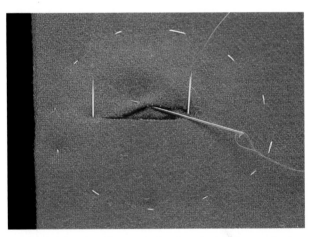

15) Finish back of buttonhole after facing is attached. Baste facing to garment around each buttonhole. Mark opening with pins; slash. Turn under; slipstitch, tucking raw edge of slit under as you sew.

How to Cord a Machine-worked Buttonhole

1) Make machine-worked buttonholes after the garment is completed. Determine buttonhole length and mark ladder, steps 1 and 2, page 117, using chalk or basting.

2) Cord with buttonhole twist placed under stitching. Leave loop at one end and tails at other. After stitching, tug on tails to hide loop. Thread tails in needle, and bring to wrong side; secure stitching in bar tack.

How to Mark the Button Placement for Single-breasted Styles

1) Line up finished front edges, facing sides together. At lower edge, buttonhole side should be slightly longer than side with buttons. Secure with pins.

2) Insert pin in buttonhole opening ⅛" (3 mm) from end closest to outer edge. Mark button placement at pin, using tailor's tack or chalk. Sew button at mark (pages 122 and 123).

How to Mark the Button Placement for Double-breasted Styles

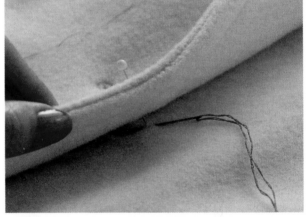

1) Lap fronts, with center front lines matching. At lower edge, overlap should be slightly longer than underlap. Secure with pins.

2) Insert pin in buttonhole opening ⅛" (3 mm) from end closest to outer edge. Carefully lift buttonhole away from pin; mark placement using tailor's tack or chalk. Sew button at mark (pages 122 and 123).

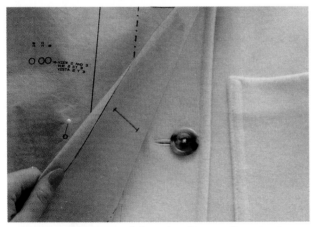

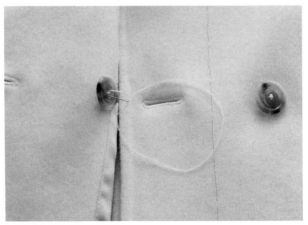

3) Use pattern to mark location for nonfunctioning button, which should line up with functioning button.

4) Mark buttonhole and button location on inside of garment under nonfunctioning button. Stitch buttonhole, then button. Or fasten with covered snap (page 123).

How to Attach a Sew-through Button

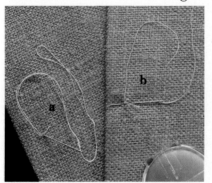

1) Cut 30" (76 cm) strand of waxed thread. Fold thread in half, and insert in eye of needle **(a)**. Or use a 15" (38 cm) single strand of waxed buttonhole twist **(b)**. Secure thread with small stitch at button placement mark.

2) Bring needle up through one hole in button, and place a toothpick across button between holes. Take three or four stitches through holes, with stitches parallel to buttonhole opening. Bring needle and thread to right side under button.

3) Remove toothpick, and lift button away from fabric so stitches are tight against button. Wind thread around stitches several times to form shank. Secure thread on right side with several small stitches close to shank. Clip thread close to stitches.

Attaching a Button with a Shank

Secure thread with small stitch at button placement mark. Stitch through shank several times, with shank parallel to buttonhole opening. Secure thread on right side with several small stitches close to shank. Clip thread close to stitches.

Reinforcing a Button

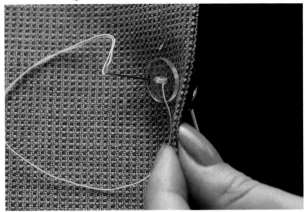

Reinforce buttons on garments that will receive a lot of wear. On facing side, position a small, flat two-hole or four-hole button under the garment button. Stitch through both buttons; form a shank under garment button.

How to Cover and Attach a Snap

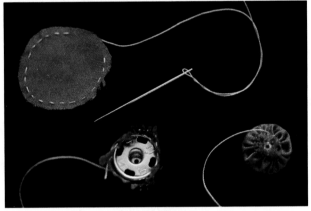

1) **Cut** two lining circles slightly larger than snap. Make small running stitches around outer edge. Place snap face down on circle; draw up stitches.

2) **Secure** thread with small stitches. Snap covered sections together; this will cut fabric and expose ball of snap. Apply liquid fray preventer to raw edges.

3) **Position** ball half of snap on facing side of overlap at desired location. Make several stitches through holes, using two strands of waxed thread; do not catch right side of garment in stitches. Secure thread with small stitches close to snap.

4) **Rub** ball of snap with chalk, and press firmly against right side of underlap to mark position for socket half. Stitch in place as for ball half, step 3, except stitch through all layers of fabric.

Index